LOW FAT
LOW CAL

LOW FAT
LOW CAL

COLLINS & BROWN

The expression Good Housekeeping as used in the
title of the book is the trademark of The National
Magazine Company and The Hearst Corporation,
registered in the United Kingdom and USA, and
other principal countries of the world, and is the
absolute property of The National Magazine
Company and The Hearst Corporation. The use
of this trademark other than with the express
permission of The National Magazine Company
or The Hearst Corporation is strictly prohibited.

The Good Housekeeping website is
www.goodhousekeeping.co.uk

ISBN 978-1-908449-98-6

A catalogue record for this book is available from
the British Library.

Reproduction by Dot Gradations Ltd, UK
Printed and bound by
1010 Printing International Ltd, China

This book can be ordered direct from the publisher.
Contact the marketing department, but try your
bookshop first.

www.anovabooks.com

NOTES

Both metric and imperial measures are given for
the recipes. Follow either set of measures, not a
mixture of both, as they are not interchangeable.

All spoon measures are level.
1 tsp = 5ml spoon; 1 tbsp = 15ml spoon.

Ovens and grills must be preheated to the specified
temperature.

Medium eggs should be used except where
otherwise specified. Free-range eggs are
recommended.

Note that some recipes contain raw or lightly
cooked eggs. The young, elderly, pregnant women
and anyone with an immune-deficiency disease
should avoid these because of the slight risk of
salmonella.

Contents

Bright Breakfasts

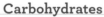

Carbohydrates

Carbohydrates provide the body with the most readily accessible form of energy. Carbohydrates in the form of sugars are found in fruit, milk and sugar; starch carbohydrates are familiar in cereals, pasta, rice, potatoes, bread and pulses. In a healthy diet, starch carbohydrates supply a higher proportion of energy than fats or sugar carbohydrates.

With the recent craze for low-carbohydrate diets, you may be forgiven for thinking that carbohydrates are best avoided. In fact, this couldn't be further from the truth. Most nutritionists agree that foods in this group are an important part of a healthy balanced diet. However, not all carbs are equal. Most of the vitamins and protective components in grains are concentrated in the bran and germ layers of the grain, but when grains are refined, as for instance in the production of white flour, the bran and germ are removed and most of the fibre and some of the nutrients are stripped away. This is why it is better to choose wholegrain carbohydrates such as brown rice and wholemeal bread over refined carbohydrates. Studies have shown that diets rich in wholegrain foods can reduce the risk of heart disease, stroke, certain types of cancer and Type 2 diabetes.

Nutrition labelling

The five key nutrients are calories, sugar, fat, saturated fat and salt. Two sets of guidelines that claim to help us select a healthy balanced diet are currently in use. The traffic light scheme developed by the Food Standards Agency provides information on fat, saturated fat, sugar and salt and uses a red, amber or green colour coding to indicate whether a food is high, medium or low in these nutrients. The other scheme is based on Guideline Daily Amounts (GDAs) (see page 19) and gives an indication of how many calories, fat, salt, sugar and fibre a food contains and what it contributes to the amount of that nutrient you should eat in a day. GDAs are guidelines for an average person of a healthy weight and average level of activity, and are just that – a guide, not a target. You should try to eat no more than the GDAs for sugars, fat, saturated fat and salt. The GDA values on the front of pack labels are based on the average requirements of an adult woman.

Five a day

One of the easiest ways to stay healthy is to eat plenty of fruit and vegetables. We can probably all remember being told by our parents to eat our 'greens' because they were good for us, and all the major reports on healthy eating have endorsed this good advice. It's no coincidence that in Mediterranean countries, where people eat almost twice the amount of fruit and vegetables that we do in the UK, they live longer and healthier lives. Fruit and vegetables contain an arsenal of disease-fighting compounds – vitamins, minerals, fibre and phytochemicals, which is why nutrition experts believe that they are the cornerstone of a healthy diet. Eating a diet rich in fruit and vegetables can reduce the risk of a range of medical problems, including heart disease, stroke, high blood pressure, certain types of cancer, cataracts and an eye condition called age-related macular degeneration, dementia and Alzheimer's disease.

Variety is key

Wherever we shop, most of us are lucky enough to have a wide range of different fruit and vegetables available to us, but do we really take advantage of the range? It's very easy to get stuck in a rut of buying the same things from one week to the next. Variety may be the spice of life, but it's also the key to a healthy diet and is particularly important when it comes to fruit and vegetables. Different coloured fruit and vegetables contain different vitamins, minerals and phytochemicals that help to keep you healthy in different ways, and so to make sure you get a good selection of all these nutrients you need to eat a variety of different produce. When you're buying fruit and vegetables don't just stick to your same old favourites – be adventurous and try something new. You'll find plenty of recipes to tempt you in this book.

Add colour to your meals

You probably already know that you should be eating at least five servings of fruit and vegetables a day, but did you know you should also be eating a rainbow? When you're planning meals, aim to fill your plate with colour – think of red, orange, yellow, green and purple fruit and vegetables and try to eat at least one serving from each of the colour bands every day.

Beans on Toast

Hands-on time: 5 minutes
Cooking time: about 15 minutes

1 tbsp olive oil
2 garlic cloves, finely sliced
400g can borlotti or cannellini beans, drained and rinsed
400g can chickpeas, drained and rinsed
400g can chopped tomatoes
2 fresh rosemary sprigs
4 slices sourdough or Granary bread
25g (1oz) Parmesan

1 Heat the oil in a pan over a low heat, add the garlic and cook for 1 minute, stirring gently.
2 Add the beans and chickpeas to the pan with the tomatoes and bring to the boil. Strip the leaves from the rosemary, then chop finely and add to the pan. Reduce the heat and simmer for 8–10 minutes until thickened.
3 Meanwhile, toast the bread and put on to plates. Grate the Parmesan into the bean mixture, stir once, then spoon over the bread. Serve immediately.

HEALTHY TIP

This low-GI breakfast will give you energy through until lunchtime.

Porridge with Dried Fruit

Hands-on time: 5 minutes
Cooking time: 5 minutes

200g (7oz) porridge oats
400ml (14fl oz) milk, plus extra
  to serve
75g (3oz) mixture of chopped dried
  figs, apricots and raisins

1 Put the oats into a large pan and add the milk and 400ml (14fl oz) water. Stir in the chopped figs, apricots and raisins and heat gently, stirring until the porridge thickens and the oats are cooked.

2 Divide among four bowls and serve with a splash of milk.

HEALTHY TIP

Porridge is an excellent way to start your day – it provides slow-release energy to sustain you through the morning.

Energy-boosting Muesli

🍴 **Hands-on time:** 5 minutes

500g (1lb 2oz) porridge oats
100g (3½oz) toasted almonds,
    chopped
2 tbsp pumpkin seeds
2 tbsp sunflower seeds
100g (3½oz) ready-to-eat dried
    apricots, chopped
milk or yogurt to serve

1 Mix the oats with the almonds, seeds and apricots. Store in a sealable container: it will keep for up to one month. Serve with milk or yogurt.

HEALTHY TIP

Oats contain gluten and, strictly speaking, are not suitable for coeliacs. However, because they contain a much smaller amount than wheat, rye or barley, research shows that most people with coeliac disease can safely eat moderate amounts. The oats must be from a source where there is no risk of contamination from wheat or wheat products during processing or packing. As individual tolerance to gluten varies, if you are a coeliac, seek expert advice before eating oats.

Makes 15 servings

Understanding Nutrients

A quick and easy way to assess if a food is high or low in a particular nutrient is to use the table opposite. Look at the amount of a particular nutrient per serving or per 100g (3½oz) for snacks or cooking ingredients and check the table below it to find out if it's high or low.

'We are what we eat'

Nutritionists from around the world agree that the food we eat has an important effect on our health and vitality. From the moment of conception and throughout life, diet plays a crucial role in helping us maintain health and fitness. A healthy balanced diet can protect against serious illnesses such as heart disease and cancer, increase resistance to colds and other infections, boost energy levels, help combat the stresses of modern living and also improve physical and mental performance. So, eating a diet that is healthy, varied and tasty should be everyone's aim.

To meet the criteria of being low fat and low calorie, each recipe in this book has been selected on the basis of it containing, per serving, a maximum of 10g fat and 400 calories.

Choose wisely

Our body needs over 40 different nutrients to function and stay healthy. Some, such as carbohydrates, proteins and fats, are required in relatively large amounts; others, such as vitamins, minerals and trace elements, are required in minute amounts, but are nonetheless essential for health. No single food or food group provides all the nutrients we need, which is why we need to eat a variety of different foods. Making sure your body gets all the nutrients it needs is easy if you focus on foods that are nutrient rich and dump those highly refined and processed foods that provide lots of saturated fat, sugar and calories but not much else.

	High	Low
Fat	more than 20g	less than 3g
Saturated fat	more than 5g	less than 1g
Sugar	more than 10g	less than 2g
Fibre	more than 3g	less than 0.5g
Sodium	more than 0.5g	less than 0.1g
Salt	more than 1.3g	less than 0.3g

Guideline Daily Amounts (GDAs)			
	Women	**Men**	**Children (5–10 years)**
Energy (cals)	2,000	2,500	1,800
Protein (g)	45	55	24
Carbohydrate (g)	230	300	220
Fat (g)	70	95	70
Saturated fat (g)	20	30	20
Total sugars (g)	90	120	85
Dietary fibre (g)	24	24	15
Sodium (g)	2.4	2.4	1.6
Salt	6	6	4

Apple and Almond Yogurt

Hands-on time: 5 minutes, plus overnight chilling

500g (1lb 2oz) natural yogurt
50g (2oz) each flaked almonds
   and sultanas
2 apples

1 Put the yogurt into a bowl and add the almonds and sultanas.
2 Grate the apples, add to the bowl and mix together. Chill in the fridge overnight. Use as a topping for breakfast cereal or serve as a snack.

HEALTHY TIP

Natural yogurt contains lactobacillus bacteria, which aids digestion and promotes a healthy immune system. Yogurt is also a good source of protein, vitamins and bone-strengthening calcium. The almonds add extra calcium while the apples provide useful amounts of fibre and the antioxidant quercetin.

SAVE EFFORT

An easy way to get a brand new dish is to use pears instead of apples. Replace the sultanas with dried cranberries.

Serves 4

Breakfast Bruschetta

TAKE 5

🍴 **Hands-on time:** 5 minutes
Cooking time: 5 minutes

1 ripe banana, peeled and sliced
250g (9oz) blueberries
200g (7oz) quark cheese
4 slices pumpernickel or wheat-free
    wholegrain bread
1 tbsp runny honey

1 Put the banana into a bowl with the
   blueberries. Spoon in the quark
   cheese and mix well.
2 Toast the slices of bread on
   both sides, then spread with the
   blueberry mixture. Drizzle with the
   honey and serve immediately.

HEALTHY TIP

This toasted treat is very low in
fat. Pumpernickel bread is made
from rye flour, which is rich in
fibre, iron and zinc. It has a lower
GI than bread made from wheat
flour, which means it provides
a sustained energy boost to
see you through the morning.
The blueberries are rich in
anthocyanins, which help combat
heart disease, certain cancers
and stroke.

22

Serves 4

Apple Compote

Hands-on time: 10 minutes, plus chilling
Cooking time: 5 minutes

250g (9oz) cooking apples, peeled
  and chopped
juice of ½ lemon
1 tbsp golden caster sugar
ground cinnamon

To serve
25g (1oz) raisins
25g (1oz) chopped almonds
1 tbsp natural yogurt

SAVE TIME

To microwave, put the apples,
lemon juice, sugar and water into
a microwave-proof bowl, cover
loosely with clingfilm and cook on
full power in an 850W microwave
oven for 4 minutes or until the
apples are just soft.

1 Put the apples into a pan with the
  lemon juice, sugar and 2 tbsp cold
  water. Cook gently for 5 minutes or
  until soft. Transfer to a bowl.
2 Sprinkle a little cinnamon over the
  top, then cool and chill. It will keep
  for up to three days.
3 Serve with the raisins, chopped
  almonds and yogurt.

Serves 2

Banana and Pecan Muffins

Hands-on time: 10 minutes
Cooking time: 20 minutes

275g (10oz) self-raising flour
1 tsp bicarbonate of soda
pinch of salt
3 very ripe large bananas, about 450g (1lb), peeled and mashed
125g (4oz) golden caster sugar
1 large egg
50ml (2fl oz) milk
75g (3oz) melted butter
50g (2oz) chopped roasted pecan nuts

1 Preheat the oven to 180°C (160°C fan oven) mark 4. Line a muffin tin with 12 paper muffin cases.
2 Sift together the flour, bicarbonate of soda and salt and put to one side.
3 Combine the bananas, sugar, egg and milk, then pour in the melted butter and mix well. Add to the flour mixture with the nuts, stirring quickly and gently with just a few strokes. Don't over-mix or the muffins will be tough. Half-fill the muffin cases.
4 Bake for 20 minutes or until golden and risen. Transfer to a wire rack and leave to cool.

SAVE EFFORT

The secret to really light, fluffy muffins is a light hand, so be sure to sift the flour and stir the mixture as little as possible; it's okay if it looks a little lumpy. Over-mixing will give tough, chewy results.

Makes 12

Strawberry Compote

Hands-on time: 15 minutes, plus chilling overnight
Cooking time: 10 minutes, plus cooling

175g (6oz) raspberry conserve
juice of 1 orange
juice of 1 lemon
1 tsp rose water
350g (12oz) strawberries, hulled and
   thickly sliced
150g (5oz) blueberries

1 Put the raspberry conserve into a
   pan with the orange and lemon
   juices and add 75ml (2½fl oz) boiling
   water. Stir over a low heat to dissolve
   the conserve, then leave to cool.
2 Stir in the rose water and taste – you
   may want to add a squeeze more
   lemon juice if it's too sweet. Put the
   strawberries and blueberries into a
   large serving bowl, then strain the
   raspberry conserve mixture over
   them. Cover and chill overnight.
   Remove the bowl from the fridge
   30 minutes before serving.

HEALTHY TIP

Berries are densely packed with
vitamins, antioxidants and other
phytonutrients (highly nutritious,
active compounds within a wide
range of foods that promote good
health). Berries also contain
compounds called anthocyanins
– the pigment that gives berries
their intense colour, mops up
damaging free radicals and helps
prevent cancer and heart disease.
They are also are rich in vitamin
C, which, together with the
anthocyanins, helps strengthen
blood capillaries and improve
blood flow around the body.

Exotic Fruit Salad

Hands-on time: 10 minutes

2 oranges

1 mango, peeled, stoned and chopped
(see page 167)

450g (1lb) peeled and diced fresh
pineapple (see page 166)

200g (7oz) blueberries

½ Charentais melon, cubed

grated zest and juice of 1 lime

1 Using a sharp knife, peel the
oranges, remove the pith and cut the
flesh into segments. Put into a bowl.

2 Add the mango, pineapple,
blueberries and melon to the bowl,
then add the lime zest and juice.
Mix together gently and serve
immediately.

SAVE EFFORT

An easy way to get a brand new
recipe is to use 2 papayas, peeled,
seeded and chopped, instead of the
pineapple.
Mix the seeds of 2 passion fruit
with the lime juice before adding to
the salad.

Serves 4

Tropical Fruit Pots

Hands-on time: 15 minutes
Cooking time: 5 minutes

400g can apricots in fruit juice

2 balls of preserved stem ginger in syrup, finely chopped, plus 2 tbsp syrup from the jar

½ tsp ground cinnamon

juice of 1 orange

3 oranges, cut into segments

1 mango, peeled, stoned and chopped (see page 167)

1 pineapple, peeled, core removed, and chopped (see page 166)

450g (1lb) coconut yogurt

3 tbsp lemon curd

3–4 tbsp light muscovado sugar

1 Drain the juice from the apricots into a pan and stir in the syrup from the ginger, then add the chopped ginger, the cinnamon and orange juice. Put over a low heat and stir gently. Bring to the boil, then reduce the heat and simmer for 2–3 minutes to make a thick syrup.

2 Roughly chop the apricots and put into a bowl with the segmented oranges, the mango and pineapple. Pour the syrup over the fruit. Divide among eight 300ml (½ pint) glasses or bowls.

3 Beat the yogurt and lemon curd together in a bowl until smooth. Spoon a generous dollop over the fruit and sprinkle with muscovado sugar. Chill if not serving immediately.

SAVE TIME

Complete the recipe to the end of step 2 up to 2 hours before you plan to eat – no need to chill. Complete the recipe to serve.

Serves 8

Feel-good Food

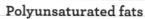

Of all the nutrients in our diet fat must be the most debated and the most misunderstood. Although, in terms of healthy eating, fat is often cast as the villain, it's worth remembering that it also plays a beneficial role. In the body, fat cushions and protects the vital organs, provides energy stores and helps insulate the body. In the diet, it is necessary for the absorption of fat-soluble vitamins (A, D, E and K) and to provide essential fatty acids that the body can't make itself. While some fat is essential, many of us are eating too much of the wrong types of fat and not enough of the right types. A high-fat diet, particularly one that contains a lot of saturated 'animal' fats, is known to increase the risk of problems such as heart disease, stroke and certain types of cancer. There are three types of fat: saturated, monounsaturated and polyunsaturated fatty acids, which occur in different proportions in foods. Saturated fatty acids are linked to higher blood cholesterol, which can then lead to heart disease.

Polyunsaturated fats

Omega-6 fats These are mostly found in vegetable oils and margarines such as sunflower oil, safflower oil, corn oil and soya bean oil. Omega-6 fats help lower the LDL ('bad') cholesterol in the blood, but if you eat too much they will also lower the 'good'.

HDL cholesterol

Omega-3 fats These are found mainly in oil-rich fish such as salmon, fresh tuna, mackerel and sardines, in linseeds (flax) and rapeseed oil. They help to protect the heart by making the blood less sticky and likely to clot, by lowering blood pressure, and by encouraging the muscles lining the artery walls to relax, thus improving blood flow to the heart. It's important to have a balance of omega-3 and omega-6 fats in the diet. At the moment most of us have too much omega-6 fats and not enough omega-3 fats and recent research suggests that low levels of omega-3s in the blood may contribute to depression, antisocial behaviour and schizophrenia.

Monounsaturated fats

Monounsaturated fats are found mainly in olive oil, walnut oil and rapeseed oil, nuts and avocados. They can help reduce the risk of heart disease by lowering LDL ('bad') cholesterol.

Saturated fats

Saturated 'animal' fats are found in full-fat dairy products (cheese, yogurt, milk, cream), lard, fatty cuts of meat and meat products such as sausages and burgers, pastry, cakes, biscuits, and coconut and palm oil. A diet high in saturated fats can raise levels of LDL ('bad') cholesterol in the blood, which will cause narrowing of the arteries and increase the risk of heart attacks and stroke.

Trans fats

Trans fats occur naturally in small amounts in meat and dairy products, but they are also produced during the process of hydrogenation that is used to convert liquid vegetable oils into semi-solid fats in the manufacture of some types of margarine. Trans fats are most commonly found in biscuits, cakes, pastries, meat pies, sausages, crackers and takeaway foods. Although, chemically, trans fats are still unsaturated fat, studies show that in the body they behave like saturated fat, causing blood cholesterol levels to rise; in fact, some studies suggest that trans fats are worse than saturated fats.

Red Lentil Soup with Low-fat Cornbread

Hands-on time: 30 minutes
Cooking time: about 30 minutes

1 tsp extra virgin olive oil, plus extra to drizzle (optional)

1 onion, roughly chopped

2 celery sticks, roughly chopped

1 garlic clove, chopped

1 tsp chilli powder (or to taste)

250g (9oz) red lentils, washed

400g can chopped tomatoes

1.1 litres (2 pints) vegetable stock

For the cornbread

100g (3½oz) plain flour

100g (3½oz) quick-cook polenta

1 tbsp caster sugar

½ tsp bicarbonate of soda

1 medium egg

175g (6oz) low-fat natural yogurt

salt

1 Start by making the soup. Heat the oil in a large pan and gently cook the onion and celery for 10 minutes until softened. Stir in the garlic and chilli powder and cook for 1 minute. Add the lentils, tomatoes and vegetable stock and bring to the boil, then reduce the heat and simmer gently for 15 minutes or until the lentils are tender.

2 Meanwhile, make the cornbread. Preheat the oven to 180°C (160°C fan oven) mark 4 and line a 450g (1lb) loaf tin with baking parchment. Measure the flour, polenta, sugar and soda into a large bowl. Add ½–¾ tsp salt (depending on taste) and whisk to combine.

3 In a separate jug, whisk together the egg and yogurt. Add to the dry ingredients and whisk until just combined. Scrape into the prepared tin, level the surface and bake for 20–25 minutes until golden and firm

38

Red lentils are a good source of
protein, fibre, iron and B vitamins.

to the touch. Leave to rest in
the tin for 10 minutes.

4 Blend the soup until smooth
(do this in batches if
necessary) and return to the
pan. Check the seasoning
(if the soup is too thick
for your liking, add a little
more water).

5 To serve, reheat the soup
(if necessary), then ladle
into warmed bowls and
drizzle with oil, if you like.
Serve with the warm sliced
cornbread.

*Serves 4
(cornbread cuts into 8 slices)*

Mozzarella Mushrooms

🍴 **Hands-on time:** 5 minutes
Cooking time: about 20 minutes

8 large portabella mushrooms
8 slices marinated red pepper
8 fresh basil leaves
150g (5oz) mozzarella cheese, cut into
  8 slices
4 English muffins, halved
salt and freshly ground black pepper
green salad to serve

1 Preheat the oven to 200°C (180°C fan oven) mark 6. Lay the mushrooms side by side in a roasting tin and season with salt and ground black pepper. Top each mushroom with a slice of red pepper and a basil leaf. Lay a slice of mozzarella on top of each mushroom and season again. Roast for 15–20 minutes until the mushrooms are tender and the cheese has melted.

2 Meanwhile, toast the muffin halves until golden. Put a mozzarella mushroom on top of each muffin half. Serve immediately with a green salad.

HEALTHY TIP

Mushrooms are an excellent source of potassium – a mineral that helps lower elevated blood pressure and reduces the risk of stroke. One medium portabella mushroom has even more potassium than a banana or a glass of orange juice. Mushrooms contain antioxidant nutrients that help inhibit the development of cancers of the breast and prostate.

Serves 4

Mexican Chicken Stew

Hands-on time: 15 minutes
Cooking time: about 30 minutes

1 tbsp olive oil

1 onion, finely sliced

3 skinless chicken breasts, cut into finger-sized strips

1 green pepper, seeded and diced

1–1½ tsp chipotle paste, to taste (see Save Effort)

1 litre (1¾ pints) chicken stock

100g (3½oz) easy-cook rice, washed

410g can black-eyed beans, drained and rinsed

a large handful of fresh coriander, roughly chopped

salt and freshly ground black pepper

To serve (optional)

low-fat soured cream

low-fat guacamole

1 Heat the oil in a large pan and fry the onion gently for 10 minutes or until softened. Add the chicken and green pepper and continue to fry for 5 minutes. Stir in the chipotle paste, stock and rice.

2 Bring the mixture to the boil, then reduce the heat and simmer for 15 minutes or until the rice is tender. Stir in the beans and most of the coriander. Check the seasoning.

3 Divide the soup among four bowls, garnish with the remaining coriander and serve with a dollop of soured cream and guacamole (to stir through), if you like.

SAVE EFFORT

The chipotle paste adds wonderful smokiness to this easy and filling stew. If you have trouble finding it, substitute with a seeded and finely chopped green chilli.

Serves 4

Understanding Salt

Reducing the amount of salt in our diet is, say health experts, one of the most important steps we can take to reduce the risk of high blood pressure, a condition that affects one in three adults in the UK.

Experts have calculated that reducing our salt intake to 6g a day would reduce the number of people suffering from stroke by 22% and from heart attacks by 16%, saving about 34,000 lives each year.

Hidden salt

You may think the easiest way to cut back on salt is not to sprinkle salt over your food when you're at the table, but unfortunately the answer isn't quite that simple – only about 15% of the salt we eat comes from salt added to our food during cooking and at the table. Three-quarters of all the salt we consume is hidden in processed foods – one small can of chicken soup, for instance, can contain well over half the recommended daily intake of salt for an adult.

Re-educating our taste buds

Our taste for salt is something we learn to like the more we eat. But just in the same way that we can teach our taste buds to enjoy foods with less sugar, we can train them to enjoy foods with less salt (sodium chloride). If you gradually reduce the amount of salt you eat, the taste receptors on the tongue become more sensitive to salt. This process takes between two and three weeks. Use herbs and spices to enhance the natural flavours of foods and before long you'll be enjoying the real taste of food – not the flavour of salt.

Fish Curry

Hands-on time: 20 minutes
Cooking time: about 25 minutes

1 tsp vegetable oil

2 onions, finely sliced

5cm (2in) piece fresh root ginger, peeled and grated

1 tsp each ground turmeric and coriander

1 tbsp medium curry paste

4 tomatoes, roughly chopped

400ml (14fl oz) fish stock

200g (7oz) raw shelled king prawns

300g (11oz) white skinless fish, such as cod, haddock, coley or pollack, cut into 2.5cm (1in) cubes

200g (7oz) frozen peas

salt and freshly ground black pepper

boiled rice or crusty bread to serve (optional)

1 Heat the oil in a large pan over a low heat. Add the onions and a good pinch of salt, then cover and cook for 15 minutes until completely softened. Stir in the ginger, turmeric, coriander and curry paste and cook for 1 minute.

2 Stir in the tomatoes and stock and simmer for 5 minutes. Mix in the prawns, fish and peas, then cook for 3–5 minutes (stirring carefully to prevent the fish from breaking up) until the prawns are bright pink and the fish is opaque. Check the seasoning and serve with rice or crusty bread, if you like.

HEALTHY TIP

If you're trying to up your veg intake, fold through a few large handfuls of spinach just before serving.

Serves 4

Chilli Crab Noodles

Hands-on time: 10 minutes
Cooking time: about 15 minutes

200g (7oz) medium egg noodles
1 tbsp vegetable oil
400g (14oz) frozen mixed vegetables
6 tbsp sweet chilli sauce
1 tbsp soy sauce
½ tbsp cornflour
100ml (3½ fl oz) chicken or
  vegetable stock
170g canned crab, drained
frozen or chopped fresh coriander
  leaves, (optional)

1 Bring a pan of water to the boil and cook the noodles according to the pack instructions. Drain well and put to one side.
2 Heat the oil in a large wok until smoking. Add the mixed vegetables and stir-fry for 5 minutes or until piping hot.
3 In a small bowl, stir together the sweet chilli sauce, soy, cornflour and stock. Add the sauce to the wok; bubble for 1 minute, then toss through the noodles, crab and coriander, if you like. Check the seasoning and serve immediately.

SAVE MONEY AND TIME

If you don't have canned crab, any canned fish or fresh or frozen seafood would work just as well.

Serves 4

Steamed Fish and Vegetable Parcels

Hands-on time: 15 minutes
Cooking time: 20 minutes

1 lemon
40g (1½oz) butter, softened
400g can cannellini beans, drained and rinsed
1 fennel bulb, thinly sliced
1 courgette, peeled into ribbons
4 × 125g (4oz) boneless, skinless white fish fillets, such as haddock, pollack or coley
8 small fresh dill sprigs
salt and freshly ground black pepper
green salad and crusty bread to serve

1 Preheat the oven to 200°C (180°C fan oven) mark 6. Cut four rough 38cm (15in) squares of baking parchment.
2 Grate the zest from the lemon, then put it into a small bowl with the butter and plenty of seasoning. Stir to combine, then set aside. Slice the zested lemon into thin rounds.
3 On one half of each square, pile a quarter of each of the beans, fennel and courgette. Top each pile with a fish fillet, then top with some lemon slices. Dollop a quarter of the butter on to each pile of vegetables and fish, then add the dill sprigs and some seasoning. Spoon 2 tbsp water on to each pile. Seal the parcels by pulling the paper up and over the filling, then folding the edges.
4 Put the parcels on baking sheets and cook in the oven for 18–20 minutes. To test whether the fish is cooked without opening the parcel, press the fish gently through the paper – it should feel as if it is flaking. Transfer the parcels to plates and bring to the table with some salad, and bread to mop up the juices.

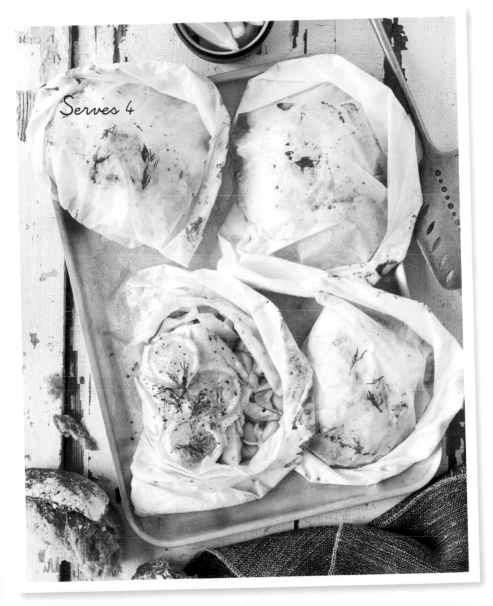

Serves 4

Sardines on Toast

Hands-on time: 5 minutes
Cooking time: about 10 minutes

4 thick slices wholemeal bread
2 large tomatoes, sliced
2 × 120g cans sardines in olive oil,
   drained
juice of ½ lemon
freshly ground black pepper
a small handful of fresh parsley,
   chopped, to garnish

SAVE EFFORT

An easy way to get a brand new
recipe is to use a 200g can salmon
in oil instead of the sardines.

1 Preheat the grill. Toast the bread on
both sides.
2 Divide the tomato slices and the
sardines among the toast slices,
squeeze the lemon juice over them,
then put back under the grill for 2–3
minutes to heat through. Season
with ground black pepper, then
scatter the parsley over the sardines
to garnish and serve immediately.

Serves 4

Chicken Tarragon Burgers

Hands-on time: 20 minutes, plus chilling
Cooking time: 12 minutes

225g (8oz) minced chicken
2 shallots, finely chopped
1 tbsp freshly chopped tarragon
25g (1oz) fresh breadcrumbs
1 large egg yolk
vegetable oil
salt and freshly ground black pepper
toasted burger buns, mayonnaise
   or Greek yogurt, salad leaves and
   tomato salad to serve

1 Put the chicken into a bowl with the shallots, tarragon, breadcrumbs and egg yolk. Mix well, then beat in about 75ml (2½fl oz) cold water and season with salt and ground black pepper.

2 Lightly oil a foil-lined baking sheet. Divide the chicken mixture into two or four portions (depending on how large you want the burgers) and put on the foil. Using the back of a wet spoon, flatten each portion to a thickness of 2.5cm (1in). Cover and chill for 30 minutes.

3 Preheat the barbecue or grill. If cooking on the barbecue, lift the burgers straight on to the grill rack; if cooking under the grill, slide the baking sheet under the grill. Cook the burgers for 5–6 minutes on each side until they are cooked through, then serve in a toasted burger bun with a dollop of mayonnaise or Greek yogurt, a few salad leaves and tomato salad.

Serves 2

Perfect Grains

Grains such as wheat, barley and quinoa are the edible see
different grasses. Many of these grains are available in a va
of forms; as side dishes they make good low-GI alternativ
to rice and potatoes.

Quinoa

This nutritious South American grain makes a great alternative to rice.

1 Put the quinoa in a bowl of cold water and mix well. Soak for 2 minutes, then drain.

2 Put into a pan with twice its volume of water. Bring to the boil, then reduce the heat and simmer for 20 minutes. Remove from the heat, cover and leave to stand for 10 minutes.

Pearl barley

Barley comes in several forms, s
you should check which type yo
have bought.

Pearl barley has had its outer hu
removed and needs no soaking.
Rinse the barley in cold water, th
put it into a pan with twice its vo
of water. Bring to the boil, then
reduce the heat and simmer unti
tender – 25–30 minutes.

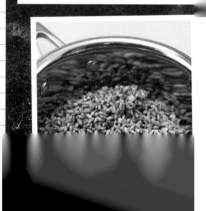

Bulgur wheat

A form of cracked wheat, bulgur has had some or all of the bran removed. It is good served as an accompaniment or used in salads. It is pre-boiled during manufacturing, and may be boiled, steamed or soaked.

Simmering bulgur Put the bulgur into a pan and add water to cover by about 2.5cm (1in). Bring to the boil, then reduce the heat and simmer for 10–15 minutes until just tender. Drain well.

Steaming bulgur Place the bulgur in a steamer lined with a clean teatowel and steam over boiling water for 20 minutes or until the grains are soft.

Soaking bulgur Put the bulgur into a deep bowl. Cover with hot water and mix with a fork. Leave to steep for 20 minutes, checking to make sure there is enough water. Drain and fluff up with a fork.

Quantities

Allow 50–75g (2–3oz) raw grain per person. Or, if measuring by volume, allow 50–75ml (2–2½fl oz).

Mild Spiced Chicken and Quinoa

Hands-on time: 15 minutes
Cooking time: about 20 minutes

2 tbsp mango chutney

juice of ½ lemon

1 tbsp olive oil

2 tsp mild curry powder

1 tsp paprika

350g (12oz) skinless chicken breast, cut into thick strips

200g (7oz) quinoa (see page 56)

1 cucumber, roughly chopped

½ bunch of spring onions, sliced

75g (3oz) ready-to-eat dried apricots, sliced

2 tbsp freshly chopped mint, basil or tarragon

salt and freshly ground black pepper

fresh mint sprigs to garnish

1 Put the chutney, lemon juice, ½ tbsp oil, the curry powder, paprika and salt and ground black pepper to taste into a bowl and mix together. Add the chicken strips and toss to coat.

2 Cook the quinoa in boiling water for 10–12 minutes until tender or according to the pack instructions. Drain thoroughly. Put into a bowl, then stir in the cucumber, spring onions, apricots, herbs and remaining oil.

3 Put the chicken and marinade into a pan and fry over a high heat for 2–3 minutes, then add 150ml (¼ pint) water. Bring to the boil, then reduce the heat and simmer for 5 minutes or until the chicken is cooked through. Serve with the quinoa garnished with mint.

Serves 4

A Month of
Healthy Eating

Monthly Meal Planner

Week 1

Tomato and Butter Bean Stew

Mushroom and Bean Hotpot

Cod with Cherry Tomatoes

Week 2

Spicy Beans with Potatoes

Cheesy Polenta with Tomato Sauce

Rich Aubergine Stew

Week 3

Courgette and Goat's Cheese Spaghetti

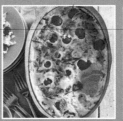

Cherry Tomato Clafoutis

Herbed Fish Crumble

Week 4

Thai Vegetable Curry

Sprouted Bean and Mango Salad

Cod Steaks with Fennel

icy Monkfish Stew

Piri Piri Chicken

Thai Green Curry

Rabbit Ragu with Pappardelle

Warm Smoked Salmon and Cucumber Salad

Prawn Gumbo

Chicken with Spicy Couscous

Beef Pho

Prawn and Pineapple Skewers

Chicken Cacciatore

Turkey Breast with Fiery Honey Sauce

Sesame Beef

Crispy Crumbed Fish

Chicken Tarragon Sweet Potatoes

Zesty Turkey One-pan

Steak and Asparagus Stir-fry

Tomato and Butter Bean Stew

Hands-on time: 10 minutes
Cooking time: about 55 minutes

2 tbsp olive oil

1 onion, finely sliced

2 garlic cloves, finely chopped

2 large leeks, trimmed and sliced

2 × 400g cans cherry tomatoes

2 × 400g cans no-added-sugar-or-salt
butter beans, drained and rinsed

150ml (¼ pint) hot vegetable stock

1–2 tbsp balsamic vinegar

salt and freshly ground black pepper

1 Preheat the oven to 180°C (160°C fan oven) mark 4. Heat the oil in a flameproof casserole over a medium heat. Add the onion and garlic and cook for 10 minutes or until golden and soft. Add the leeks, cover and cook for 5 minutes.

2 Add the tomatoes, beans and hot stock and season well with salt and ground black pepper. Bring to the boil, then cover and cook in the oven for 35–40 minutes until the sauce has thickened. Remove from the oven, stir in the vinegar and spoon into warmed bowls.

HEALTHY TIP

Butter beans provide good amounts of protein, complex carbohydrate, iron and fibre; they have a low GI so tend to release their energy over a longer period of time, keeping you feeling full longer. They are also high in potassium, which helps to regulate fluid balance in the body.

Serves 4

Mushroom and Bean Hotpot

Hands-on time: 15 minutes
Cooking time: 35 minutes

3 tbsp olive oil

700g (1½lb) chestnut mushrooms, roughly chopped

1 large onion, finely chopped

2 tbsp plain flour

2 tbsp mild curry paste (see Healthy Tip)

150ml (¼ pint) dry white wine

400g can chopped tomatoes

2 tbsp sun-dried tomato paste

2 × 400g cans mixed beans, drained and rinsed

3 tbsp mango chutney

3 tbsp roughly chopped fresh coriander and mint

1 Heat the oil in a large pan over a low heat. Add the chopped mushrooms and onion and fry until the onion is soft and dark golden. Stir in the flour and mild curry paste and cook for 1–2 minutes.

2 Add the wine, tomatoes, sun-dried tomato paste and beans and bring to the boil, then reduce the heat and simmer gently for 30 minutes or until most of the liquid has reduced. Stir in the mango chutney and chopped herbs before serving.

HEALTHY TIP

Beans are rich in protein, fibre and many vitamins and minerals. They have been linked with a reduced risk of cancers of the breast, prostate and colon, as well as heart disease and Type 2 diabetes.

Check the ingredients in the curry paste: some pastes may not be suitable for vegetarians.

Serves 6

Cod with Cherry Tomatoes

Hands-on time: 15 minutes
Cooking time: about 25 minutes

4 × 100g (3½oz) cod steaks
1 tbsp plain flour
2 tbsp olive oil
1 small onion, sliced
1 large red chilli, seeded and chopped
   (see Safety Tip)
1 garlic clove, crushed
250g (9oz) cherry tomatoes, halved
4 spring onions, chopped
2 tbsp freshly chopped coriander
salt and freshly ground black pepper

1 Season the cod with salt and ground black pepper, then dust lightly with the flour. Heat 1 tbsp oil in a large frying pan over a medium heat. Add the onion and fry gently for 5–10 minutes until golden.

2 Pour the remaining oil into the pan. Add the cod and fry for 3 minutes on each side. Add the chilli, garlic, cherry tomatoes, spring onions and coriander and season with salt and ground black pepper. Cover and continue to cook for 5–10 minutes until everything is heated through. Serve immediately.

SAFETY TIP

Chillies can be quite mild to blisteringly hot, depending on the type of chilli and its ripeness. Taste a small piece first to check it's not too hot for you. Be extremely careful when handling chillies not to touch or rub your eyes with your fingers, or they will sting. Wash knives immediately after handling chillies. As a precaution, use rubber gloves when preparing them, if you like.

Serves 4

Spicy Monkfish Stew

Hands-on time: 10 minutes
Cooking time: 35 minutes

1 tbsp olive oil

1 onion, finely sliced

1 tbsp tom yum paste (see Save Time)

450g (1lb) potatoes, cut into 2cm (¾in) chunks

400g can chopped tomatoes in rich tomato juice

600ml (1 pint) hot fish stock

450g (1lb) monkfish, cut into 2cm (¾in) chunks

200g (7oz) ready-to-eat baby spinach

salt and freshly ground black pepper

1 Heat the oil in a pan over a medium heat. Add the onion and fry for 5 minutes or until golden.

2 Add the tom yum paste and potatoes and stir-fry for 1 minute. Add the tomatoes and hot stock, season well with salt and ground black pepper and cover the pan. Bring to the boil, then reduce the heat and simmer, partially covered, for 15 minutes or until the potatoes are just tender.

3 Add the monkfish to the pan and continue to simmer for 5–10 minutes until the fish is cooked. Add the spinach and stir through until wilted. Spoon the fish stew into warmed bowls and serve immediately.

SAVE TIME

Tom yum paste is a hot and spicy Thai mixture used in soups and stews. It is available from large supermarkets and Asian food shops.

Serves 6

Piri Piri Chicken

Hands-on time: 15 minutes
Cooking time: about 45 minutes

1 red onion, cut into 8 wedges
1 tbsp olive oil
4 skinless chicken breasts
1 each red and yellow pepper, seeded
　　and cut into strips
a large handful of fresh coriander or
　　parsley, roughly chopped, to garnish
boiled rice or green salad to serve

For the sauce

1 red onion, roughly chopped
2 garlic cloves, roughly chopped
1 red chilli, seeded and roughly
　　chopped (see Safety Tip, page 68)
½ tsp smoked paprika
juice of 1 lemon
1 tbsp white wine vinegar
1 tbsp Worcestershire sauce
salt and freshly ground black pepper

1 Preheat the oven to 200°C (180°C fan oven) mark 6. Put the onion wedges in a medium roasting tin or ovenproof serving dish (just large enough to hold the chicken breasts in a single layer), add the oil and toss through. Put into the oven to roast for 15 minutes.

2 While the onions are roasting, make the sauce. Put all the ingredients into a blender and whiz until smooth. Put to one side.

3 Slash the top of each chicken breast to allow the flavours to penetrate. Carefully take the onion tin out of the oven, then add the chicken, sauce and peppers and gently toss everything together to mix. Rearrange the chicken in the tin, cut side up.

4 Cook for 25–30 minutes until the chicken is cooked through. Garnish with coriander or parsley and serve with rice or a green salad.

Serves 4

Thai Green Curry

Hands-on time: 15 minutes
Cooking time: about 15 minutes

2 tsp vegetable oil

1 green chilli, seeded and finely
   chopped (see Safety Tip, page 68)

4cm (1½in) piece fresh root ginger,
   peeled and finely grated

1 lemongrass stalk, trimmed and cut
   into three pieces

225g (8oz) brown-cap or oyster
   mushrooms

1 tbsp Thai green curry paste

300ml (½ pint) coconut milk

150ml (¼ pint) chicken stock

1 tbsp Thai fish sauce

1 tsp light soy sauce

350g (12oz) boneless, skinless chicken
   breasts, cut into bite-size pieces

350g (12oz) cooked peeled king
   prawns

fresh coriander sprigs to garnish

Thai fragrant rice to serve

1 Heat the oil in a wok or large frying pan. Add the chilli, ginger, lemongrass and mushrooms and stir-fry for about 3 minutes until the mushrooms begin to turn golden. Add the curry paste and fry for a further 1 minute.

2 Pour in the coconut milk, stock, fish sauce and soy sauce and bring to the boil. Stir in the chicken, then reduce the heat and simmer for about 8 minutes until the chicken is cooked.

3 Add the prawns and cook for a further 1 minute. Garnish with coriander sprigs and serve immediately, with Thai fragrant rice.

Serves 6

Rabbit Ragu with Pappardelle

Hands-on time: 25 minutes
Cooking time: about 1¼ hours

450g (1lb) diced rabbit meat (ask your butcher or order via your supermarket)

1 tbsp plain flour

1 tbsp olive oil

1 onion, finely chopped

2 celery sticks, finely chopped

1 large carrot, finely chopped

2 rosemary sprigs

1 bay leaf

2 tbsp tomato purée

450ml (¾ pint) chicken stock

400g can chopped tomatoes

200g (7oz) dried pappardelle pasta

salt and freshly ground black pepper

1 Dry the rabbit pieces roughly with kitchen paper and sprinkle over the flour. Heat the oil in a large pan, add the rabbit, onion, celery and carrot. Fry for 5 minutes, adding a little water if the pan gets dry.

2 Add the rosemary, bay leaf, tomato purée, stock, tomatoes and plenty of seasoning. Bring to the boil, reduce the heat, cover and simmer for 45 minutes. Take off the lid and simmer for a further 15 minutes, stirring occasionally.

3 When the rabbit has 15 minutes left to cook, bring a large pan of salted water to the boil and cook the pasta according to the pack instructions. Drain the pasta.

4 Check the seasoning of the ragu and serve immediately with pasta.

HEALTHY TIP

Rabbit is lean, so ideal when you are watching calories. Use chicken thighs if you like (they need less cooking).

Serves 6

Week 1 - Shopping List

CHILLED & FROZEN
- ☐ 4 skinless chicken breasts
- ☐ 350g (12oz) boneless, skinless chicken breasts
- ☐ 450 g (1lb) diced rabbit meat
- ☐ 450g (1lb) monkfish
- ☐ 4 × 100g (3½oz) cod steaks
- ☐ 350g (12oz) cooked peeled king prawns

FRUIT, VEG & HERBS
- ☐ 5 onions
- ☐ 2 red onions
- ☐ 1 garlic bulb
- ☐ 1 red pepper
- ☐ 1 yellow pepper
- ☐ 1 carrot
- ☐ 1 pack celery
- ☐ 450g (1lb) potatoes
- ☐ 225g (8oz) brown-cap (or oyster) mushrooms
- ☐ 700g (1½lb) chestnut mushrooms
- ☐ 250g (9oz) cherry tomatoes
- ☐ 2 large leeks
- ☐ 200g (7oz) baby spinach
- ☐ 2 red chillies
- ☐ 1 green chilli
- ☐ 4 spring onions
- ☐ Fresh root ginger
- ☐ 1 lemon
- ☐ 1 lemongrass stalk
- ☐ Pack of fresh coriander
- ☐ Pack of fresh parsley

STORECUPBOARD

(Here's a checklist in case you need
to re-stock)

- ❏ Vegetable oil
- ❏ Olive oil
- ❏ Vegetable stock
- ❏ Fish stock
- ❏ Chicken stock
- ❏ Plain flour
- ❏ 2 × 400g cans mixed beans
- ❏ 3 × 400g cans chopped tomatoes
- ❏ 2 × 400g cans cherry tomatoes
- ❏ 2 × 400g cans no-added-sugar-or-salt butter beans
- ❏ Balsamic vinegar
- ❏ White wine vinegar
- ❏ Worcestershire sauce
- ❏ Thai fish sauce
- ❏ Light soy sauce
- ❏ Mild curry paste
- ❏ Tom yum paste
- ❏ Thai green curry paste
- ❏ Tomato purée
- ❏ Sun-dried tomato paste
- ❏ Coconut milk
- ❏ Smoked paprika
- ❏ Bay leaves
- ❏ Mango chutney
- ❏ 150ml (¼ pint) dry white wine
- ❏ Pappardelle pasta
- ❏ Thai fragrant rice
- ❏ Rice, to serve

Spicy Beans with Potatoes

Hands-on time: 12 minutes
Cooking time: about 1½ hours

4 baking potatoes
1 tbsp olive oil, plus extra to rub
1 tsp smoked paprika, plus a pinch
2 shallots, finely chopped
1 tbsp freshly chopped rosemary
400g can cannellini beans, drained
    and rinsed
400g can chopped tomatoes
1 tbsp light muscovado sugar
1 tsp Worcestershire sauce
75ml (2½fl oz) red wine
75ml (2½fl oz) hot vegetable stock
a small handful of freshly chopped
    flat-leafed parsley
grated mature Cheddar to sprinkle
sea salt and freshly ground black
    pepper

1 Preheat the oven to 200°C (180°C fan oven) mark 6. Rub the potatoes with a little oil and put them on a baking tray. Scatter with sea salt and a pinch of smoked paprika and bake for 1–1½ hours.

2 Meanwhile, heat the 1 tbsp oil in a large pan, then fry the shallots over a low heat for 1–2 minutes until they start to soften.

3 Add the rosemary and 1 tsp paprika and fry for 1–2 minutes, then add the beans, tomatoes, sugar, Worcestershire sauce, wine and hot stock. Season, then bring to the boil, reduce the heat and simmer, uncovered, for 10–15 minutes. Serve with the baked potatoes, scattered with parsley and grated Cheddar.

SAVE EFFORT

For a quick meal that takes less than 25 minutes, the spicy beans are just as good served with toast.

Serves 4

Cheesy Polenta with Tomato Sauce

Hands-on time: 15 minutes, plus cooling
Cooking time: 40 minutes

a little vegetable oil

225g (8oz) polenta

4 tbsp freshly chopped herbs, such as oregano, chives and flat-leafed parsley

100g (3½oz) freshly grated Parmesan, plus fresh Parmesan shavings to serve

salt and freshly ground black pepper

For the tomato and basil sauce

1 tbsp vegetable oil

3 garlic cloves, crushed

500g carton creamed tomatoes or passata

1 bay leaf

1 fresh thyme sprig

a large pinch of caster sugar

3 tbsp freshly chopped basil, plus extra to garnish

1 Lightly oil a 25.5 × 18cm (10 × 7in) dish. Bring 1.1 litres (2 pints) water and ¼ tsp salt to the boil in a large pan. Sprinkle in the polenta, whisking constantly. Reduce the heat and simmer, stirring frequently, for 10–15 minutes until the mixture leaves the sides of the pan.

2 Stir in the herbs and Parmesan and season to taste with salt and ground black pepper. Turn into the prepared dish and leave to cool.

3 Next, make the tomato and basil sauce. Heat the oil in a pan and fry the garlic for 30 seconds (do not brown). Add the creamed tomatoes or passata, the bay leaf, thyme and sugar. Season with salt and ground black pepper and bring to the boil, then reduce the heat and simmer, uncovered, for 5–10 minutes. Remove the bay leaf and thyme sprig and add the chopped basil.

SAVE TIME

Complete the recipe to the end of
step 3. Cover and chill separately
for up to two days. Complete the
recipe to serve.

4 To serve, preheat a
griddle or grill. Cut the
polenta into pieces and
lightly brush with oil.
Fry on the hot griddle
for 3–4 minutes on each
side, or under the hot
grill for 7–8 minutes on
each side. Serve with the
tomato and basil sauce,
fresh Parmesan shavings
and chopped basil.

Serves 6

Rich Aubergine Stew

Hands-on time: 25 minutes
Cooking time: about 30 minutes

1 tbsp extra virgin olive oil, plus extra to drizzle

3 medium aubergines, cut into 2.5cm (1in) pieces

1 onion, roughly chopped

2 celery sticks, roughly chopped

1 red pepper, seeded and roughly chopped

400g can chopped tomatoes

100g (3½oz) green olives, pitted

1 tsp caster sugar

1 tbsp red wine vinegar

a large handful of fresh parsley, chopped

50g (2oz) raisins (optional)

salt and freshly ground black pepper

crusty bread to serve

1 Heat the oil in a large pan and cook the aubergines for 10–12 minutes until brown and almost tender. Add the onion, celery, red pepper and a splash of water and fry for 5 minutes.

2 Add the tomatoes, olives and some seasoning and simmer for 10 minutes or until the aubergine is completely tender.

3 Stir in the sugar, vinegar, parsley and the raisins, if you like. Drizzle with extra oil, if you like, and serve warm or at room temperature with some crusty bread.

SAVE EFFORT

Aubergines take a little longer to cook than you might think, so make sure they are succulently soft before serving this vegetarian dish.

Serves 4

Warm Smoked Salmon and Cucumber Salad

🍴 **Hands-on time:** 10 minutes
Cooking time: about 5 minutes

½ tbsp vegetable oil
2.5cm (1in) piece fresh root ginger, peeled and finely chopped
1 green chilli, seeded and finely chopped (see Safety Tip, page 68)
1 tbsp sesame seeds
6 baby sweetcorn, finely sliced
300g (11oz) straight-to-wok rice noodles
1 cucumber, peeled into ribbons
1 tbsp toasted sesame oil
1 tbsp light soy sauce
120g pack smoked salmon trimmings
salt and freshly ground black pepper
a large handful of fresh coriander, finely chopped, to garnish
lime wedges to serve

1 Heat the vegetable oil in a large frying pan or wok. Add the ginger, chilli and sesame seeds and cook for 1 minute. Stir in the baby sweetcorn and noodles and cook, stirring frequently, for 3 minutes or until the noodles are tender.

2 Add the cucumber, sesame oil, soy sauce and smoked salmon trimmings and heat through. Check the seasoning. Garnish with coriander and serve immediately with lime wedges to squeeze over.

HEALTHY TIP

Ginger is a good digestive aid and useful for alleviating and preventing travel sickness.

Serves 4

Prawn Gumbo

Hands-on time: 20 minutes
Cooking time: about 50 minutes

1 tbsp vegetable oil

1 medium onion, finely sliced

2 celery sticks, finely chopped

2 green peppers, seeded and roughly
   chopped

1–2 red chillies, to taste, seeded and
   finely chopped (see Safety Tip,
   page 68)

3 fresh thyme sprigs

2 garlic cloves, crushed

2 × 400g cans chopped tomatoes

1 litre (1¾ pints) vegetable stock

200g (7oz) okra, roughly chopped

150g (5oz) basmati rice, washed and
   drained

300g (11oz) cooked peeled king
   prawns

salt and freshly ground black pepper

a large handful of fresh flat-leafed
   parsley, roughly chopped, to garnish

1 Heat the oil in a large frying pan
   and fry the onion, celery and green
   peppers gently for 5 minutes or
   until beginning to soften. Stir in
   the chillies, thyme, garlic, tomatoes,
   stock and okra and bring to the boil,
   then reduce the heat and simmer for
   20 minutes.

2 Stir in the rice, reduce the heat and
   simmer for 20 minutes, stirring
   occasionally, until the rice is cooked
   and the liquid has been absorbed.

3 Stir in the prawns, heat through
   and check the seasoning. Discard
   the thyme sprigs, garnish with the
   parsley and serve.

Serves 4

Chicken with Spicy Couscous

Hands-on time: 15 minutes, plus soaking

125g (4oz) couscous

1 ripe mango, peeled, stoned and cut into 2.5cm (1in) chunks (see page 167)

1 tbsp lemon or lime juice

125g tub fresh tomato salsa

3 tbsp mango chutney

3 tbsp orange juice

2 tbsp freshly chopped coriander, plus extra to garnish

200g (7oz) chargrilled chicken fillets

4 tbsp fromage frais (optional)

salt and freshly ground black pepper

lime wedges to serve

1 Put the couscous into a large bowl and pour 300ml (½ pint) boiling water over it. Season well with salt and ground black pepper, then leave to soak for 15 minutes.

2 Put the mango chunks on a large plate and sprinkle with the lemon or lime juice.

3 Mix the tomato salsa with the mango chutney, orange juice and coriander in a small bowl.

4 Drain the couscous if necessary, fluff the grains with a fork, then stir in the salsa mixture and check the seasoning. Turn out on to a large serving dish and arrange the chicken and mango on top.

5 Just before serving, spoon the fromage frais over the chicken, if you like, then garnish with chopped coriander, and serve with lime wedges to squeeze over.

Serves 4

Beef Pho

Hands-on time: 15 minutes
Cooking time: about 25 minutes

1 tbsp vegetable oil

400g (14oz) sirloin steak, excess fat trimmed

1.6 litres (2¾ pints) beef stock

1 star anise

4 whole cloves

1 cinnamon stick

1 tbsp each soy and fish sauce, plus extra to taste

150g (5oz) rice noodles

1 onion, very thinly sliced

225g (8oz) bean sprouts

1 red chilli, seeded and sliced into rings (see Safety Tip, page 68)

a small handful each of fresh basil and coriander, chopped

salt and freshly ground black pepper

lime wedges to serve

1 Heat the oil in a large frying pan over a high heat. Pat the steak dry with kitchen paper, season well and fry for 5–6 minutes, turning once, for medium meat (cook for shorter/longer if you prefer). Lift the steaks out of the frying pan and put to one side on a board.

2 Pour the stock into a separate large pan, add the spices and bring to the boil, then reduce the heat and simmer for 5 minutes. Add the soy sauce, fish sauce and noodles and cook for 5 minutes, then add the onion, bean sprouts and chilli. Take off the heat.

3 Slice the steak into thin strips. Divide the soup among four large bowls. Add a quarter of the beef strips to each bowl and sprinkle with the herbs. Serve with lime wedges to squeeze over.

Serves 4

Week 2 - Shopping List

CHILLED & FROZEN
- [ ] 400g (14oz) sirloin steak
- [ ] 200g (7oz) chargrilled chicken fillets
- [ ] 300g (11oz) cooked peeled king prawns
- [ ] 120g pack smoked salmon trimmings
- [ ] 125g (4oz) Parmesan
- [ ] Mature Cheddar (to sprinkle)
- [ ] 60g (2½oz) fromage frais
- [ ] 125g tub fresh tomato salsa

FRUIT, VEG & HERBS
- [ ] 3 onions
- [ ] 2 shallots
- [ ] 1 garlic bulb
- [ ] 1 red pepper
- [ ] 2 green peppers
- [ ] 1 head of celery
- [ ] 3 red chillies
- [ ] 1 green chilli
- [ ] 3 medium aubergines
- [ ] 4 baking potatoes
- [ ] 1 cucumber
- [ ] Fresh root ginger
- [ ] 3 limes
- [ ] 6 baby sweetcorn
- [ ] 200g (7oz) okra
- [ ] 225g (8oz) bean sprouts
- [ ] Pack of fresh rosemary
- [ ] Pack of fresh thyme
- [ ] Pack of fresh basil
- [ ] Pack of fresh coriander
- [ ] 2 × packs of fresh flat-leafed parsley
- [ ] 1 ripe mango

STORECUPBOARD

(Here's a checklist in case you need
to re-stock)

- ❏ Vegetable oil
- ❏ Olive oil
- ❏ Extra virgin olive oil
- ❏ Toasted sesame oil
- ❏ Beef stock
- ❏ Vegetable stock
- ❏ 4 × 400g cans chopped tomatoes
- ❏ 500g carton creamed tomatoes or passata
- ❏ 400g can cannellini beans
- ❏ 100g (3½oz) pitted green olives
- ❏ Red wine vinegar
- ❏ Fish sauce
- ❏ Soy sauce
- ❏ Worcestershire sauce
- ❏ 50g (2oz) raisins
- ❏ Smoked paprika
- ❏ Star anise
- ❏ Cinnamon stick
- ❏ Cloves
- ❏ Bay leaves
- ❏ Sesame seeds
- ❏ Mango chutney
- ❏ Caster sugar
- ❏ Light muscovado sugar
- ❏ Lemon (or lime) juice
- ❏ Orange juice
- ❏ 75ml (2½fl oz) red wine
- ❏ Straight-to-wok noodles
- ❏ Rice noodles, to serve
- ❏ 225g (8oz) polenta
- ❏ Couscous
- ❏ Basmati rice
- ❏ Crusty bread, to serve

Courgette and Goat's Cheese Spaghetti

Hands-on time: 10 minutes
Cooking time: about 10 minutes

350g (12oz) dried spaghetti
1 tbsp olive oil
1 garlic clove, finely chopped
½–1 red chilli, to taste, seeded and finely chopped (see Safety Tip, page 68)
2 medium courgettes, coarsely grated
finely grated zest and juice of 1 lemon
75g (3oz) soft, crumbly goat's cheese
a small handful of fresh mint, finely shredded
salt and freshly ground black pepper

1 Cook the spaghetti in a large pan of boiling water according to the pack instructions.

2 Meanwhile, heat the oil in a large frying pan, add the garlic and chilli and fry for 30 seconds, then add the courgettes and fry for a further 1 minute. Put to one side.

3 When the pasta is cooked to your liking, reserve a cupful of the cooking water before draining. Add the drained pasta to the courgette pan together with the lemon zest and juice. Crumble in most of the goat's cheese, then toss to combine, adding some of the reserved pasta water if the mixture seems dry.

4 Check the seasoning, then divide among four bowls. Sprinkle with the mint, the remaining goat's cheese and plenty of pepper. Serve immediately.

HEALTHY TIP

Goat's cheese is lower in fat and has fewer calories than cow's milk cheese.

Serves 4

Cherry Tomato Clafoutis

Hands-on time: 10 minutes
Cooking time: about 30 minutes

60g (2½oz) plain flour

1 tsp baking powder

3 large eggs

100ml (3½fl oz) semi-skimmed milk

3 tbsp shredded fresh basil, plus extra
   whole leaves to garnish

150g (5oz) cottage cheese

250g (9oz) cherry tomatoes

salt and freshly ground black pepper

green salad to serve

1 Preheat the oven to 180°C (160°C fan oven) mark 4. Put the flour, baking powder, eggs, milk and plenty of seasoning into a food processor and whiz until the mixture is smooth (alternatively, put all the ingredients into a large bowl and whisk together by hand). Empty the mixture into a bowl and whisk in the shredded basil and the cottage cheese.

2 Pour the mixture into a 1 litre (1¾ pint) shallow ovenproof serving dish, then drop in the cherry tomatoes. Season with ground black pepper.

3 Cook for 30 minutes or until the egg is golden and has set (a knife inserted into the mixture should come out clean). Garnish with extra basil leaves and serve immediately with a crisp green salad.

SAVE EFFORT

This recipe is extremely versatile – try adding a handful of torn ham, spring onions or any soft herb you like.

Herbed Fish Crumble

🍴 **Hands-on time:** 15 minutes
🍴 **Cooking time:** about 40 minutes

1½ tbsp olive oil

1 onion, finely chopped

1 fennel bulb, finely chopped

2 × 400g cans chopped tomatoes

2 tsp dried basil

150g (5oz) ciabatta bread, torn into
rough pieces

a large handful of fresh parsley,
chopped

500g (1lb 2oz) skinless white fish, such
as cod, coley, haddock or pollack,
diced

salt and freshly ground black pepper

green salad to serve

1 Heat ½ tbsp oil in a large frying
pan and fry the onion and fennel
gently for 8 minutes or until
beginning to soften.

2 Add the tomatoes and basil and
bring to the boil, then reduce the
heat and simmer for 10–15 minutes
until the sauce is pulpy and thick.

3 Meanwhile, preheat the oven to
220°C (200°C fan oven) mark 7. Put
the ciabatta pieces, the remaining
oil and half the parsley into a large
bowl and stir to combine.

4 Add the fish to the tomato sauce
and cook for 5 minutes or until
just cooked. Stir in the remaining
parsley and check the seasoning,
then spoon the mixture into a 2 litre
(3½ pint) ovenproof dish. Cover with
the bread topping and bake for 10–12
minutes until bubbling and golden
on top. Serve with a green salad.

Serves 4

Prawn and Pineapple Skewers

Hands-on time: 15 minutes
Cooking time: about 10 minutes

300g (11oz) raw peeled king prawns

400g (14oz) fresh pineapple chunks
(see page 166)

2 red peppers, seeded and cut into 4cm
(1½in) chunks

½ tbsp vegetable oil

grated zest and juice of 2 limes, plus
extra wedges to serve

1 tsp fish sauce

1 tbsp runny honey

2cm (¾in) piece fresh root ginger,
peeled and grated

1 garlic clove, finely chopped

½–1 red chilli, to taste, seeded and
finely chopped (see Safety Tip,
page 68)

freshly ground black pepper

boiled rice to serve

1 Soak 12 wooden skewers in hot water for 5 minutes. Preheat the grill to medium.

2 Divide the prawns, pineapple and pepper chunks among the presoaked skewers. Arrange the skewers on a baking sheet, brush with oil and grill for 3 minutes on each side or until the prawns have turned pink and the pineapple and peppers have just started to colour.

3 Stir the remaining ingredients (except the ground black pepper) together in a small bowl, then brush a little of the sauce over the cooked skewers. Season the skewers with pepper, then serve with boiled rice, lime wedges to squeeze over and the remaining sauce as a dip.

Serves 4

Chicken Cacciatore

Hands-on time: 10 minutes
Cooking time: about 30 minutes

1 tbsp olive oil

4 skinless chicken breasts

1 onion, chopped

250g (9oz) white mushrooms, sliced

2 × 400g cans chopped tomatoes

1 tsp dried oregano

1 bay leaf

150ml (¼ pint) chicken stock or water

a large handful of rocket

salt and freshly ground black pepper

seasonal vegetables or crusty bread
to serve

1 Heat half the oil in a large, deep frying pan. Fry the chicken over a high heat for 6 minutes, turning once. Lift the chicken out and put to one side on a plate.
2 Heat the remaining oil in the chicken pan and fry the onion and mushrooms over a medium heat for 8 minutes or until beginning to soften. Stir in the tomatoes, oregano, bay leaf and chicken stock or water, then return the chicken to the pan.

Bring the mixture to the boil, then reduce the heat and simmer for 15 minutes, turning the chicken halfway through the cooking time, until the chicken is cooked through and the sauce has thickened.
3 Remove the bay leaf, then season well and stir the rocket through. Serve with seasonal vegetables, or crusty bread to mop up the juices.

SAVE EFFORT

As an alternative, shred the chicken once cooked and return to the tomato mixture to make a hearty pasta sauce.

Serves 4

Turkey Breast with Fiery Honey Sauce

Hands-on time: 15 minutes
Cooking time: about 15 minutes

½ tbsp olive oil

4 turkey breast steaks, total weight about 500g (1lb 2oz)

1 tbsp Worcestershire sauce

½–1 red chilli, to taste, seeded and finely chopped (see Safety Tip, page 68)

1½ tbsp runny honey

100ml (3½fl oz) chicken stock

4 spring onions, finely sliced

salt and freshly ground black pepper

seasonal vegetables, cooked noodles or salad to serve

1 Heat the oil in a large frying pan over a medium-high heat and cook the turkey steaks for 8–10 minutes, turning once, until cooked through. Transfer to a board, cover well with foil to keep warm and leave to rest while you prepare the sauce.

2 Return the pan to the heat and add the Worcestershire sauce, chilli, honey, stock, spring onions and some seasoning. Heat through and leave to bubble for 2 minutes until slightly thickened.

3 Serve the turkey and sauce with some seasonal vegetables, cooked noodles or salad.

HEALTHY TIP

Lean and low in fat, turkey is also a good source of protein.

Serves 4

Sesame Beef

🍴 **Hands-on time:** 10 minutes
Cooking time: 10 minutes

2 tbsp soy sauce
2 tbsp Worcestershire sauce
2 tsp tomato purée
juice of ½ lemon
1 tbsp sesame seeds
1 garlic clove, crushed
400g (14oz) rump steak, sliced
1 tbsp vegetable oil
3 small pak choi, chopped
1 bunch of spring onions, sliced
freshly cooked egg noodles or
    tagliatelle to serve

1 Mix the soy sauce, Worcestershire
sauce, tomato purée, lemon juice,
sesame seeds and garlic together
in a bowl. Add the steak and toss·
to coat.

2 Heat the oil in a large wok or non-
stick frying pan until hot. Add the
steak and sear well. Remove from
the wok and put to one side.

3 Add any sauce from the bowl to the
wok and heat for 1 minute. Add the
pak choi, spring onions and steak
and stir-fry for 5 minutes. Add
the freshly cooked and drained
noodles or pasta, toss and serve
immediately.

SAVE EFFORT

For an easy way to get a brand
new recipe, use 400g (14oz) pork
escalope cut into strips instead of
beef. Cook for 5 minutes before
removing from the pan at step 2.

Serves 4

Week 3 - Shopping List

CHILLED & FROZEN
- ❏ 400g (14oz) rump steak
- ❏ 4 turkey breast steaks (500g/1lb 2oz total weight)
- ❏ 4 skinless chicken breasts
- ❏ 300g (11oz) raw peeled king prawns
- ❏ 500g (1lb 2oz) skinless white fish
- ❏ 3 large eggs
- ❏ 75g (3oz) crumbly goat's cheese
- ❏ 150g (5oz) cottage cheese
- ❏ 100ml (3½fl oz) semi-skimmed milk

FRUIT, VEG & HERBS
- ❏ 2 onions
- ❏ 2 bunches of spring onions
- ❏ 1 garlic bulb
- ❏ 2 red peppers
- ❏ 3 red chillies
- ❏ 1 fennel bulb
- ❏ 250g (9oz) white mushrooms
- ❏ 250g (9oz) cherry tomatoes
- ❏ 2 medium courgettes
- ❏ 3 small pak choi
- ❏ Fresh root ginger
- ❏ 2 lemons
- ❏ 3 limes
- ❏ 400g (14oz) fresh pineapple chunks
- ❏ Pack of fresh mint
- ❏ Pack of fresh basil
- ❏ Pack of fresh parsley
- ❏ Pack of fresh rocket
- ❏ Seasonal veg, to serve
- ❏ Green salad, to serve

STORECUPBOARD

(Here's a checklist in case you need to re-stock)

- ❏ Olive oil
- ❏ Vegetable oil
- ❏ Chicken stock
- ❏ Plain flour
- ❏ 4 × 400g cans chopped tomatoes
- ❏ Worcestershire sauce
- ❏ Soy sauce
- ❏ Fish sauce
- ❏ Tomato purée
- ❏ Spaghetti
- ❏ Baking powder
- ❏ Runny honey
- ❏ Dried oregano
- ❏ Dried basil
- ❏ Bay leaves
- ❏ Sesame seeds
- ❏ 150g (5oz) ciabatta bread
- ❏ Rice, to serve
- ❏ Noodles, to serve
- ❏ Tagliatelle, to serve
- ❏ Crusty bread, to serve

Thai Vegetable Curry

Hands-on time: 10 minutes
Cooking time: 15 minutes

2–3 tbsp red Thai curry paste

2.5cm (1in) piece fresh root ginger, peeled and finely chopped

50g (2oz) cashew nuts

400ml can coconut milk

3 carrots, cut into thin batons

1 broccoli head, cut into florets

20g (¾oz) fresh coriander, roughly chopped

zest and juice of 1 lime

2 large handfuls of spinach leaves

boiled basmati rice to serve

1 Put the curry paste into a large pan, add the ginger and nuts and stir-fry over a medium heat for 2–3 minutes.

2 Add the coconut milk, cover and bring to the boil. Stir the carrots into the pan, then reduce the heat and simmer for 5 minutes. Add the broccoli florets and simmer for a further 5 minutes or until tender.

3 Stir the coriander and lime zest into the pan with the spinach. Squeeze the lime juice over and serve with boiled basmati rice.

SAVE EFFORT

For an easy way to get a brand new recipe, replace the carrots and/or broccoli with alternative vegetables – try baby sweetcorn, sugarsnap peas or mangetouts and simmer for only 5 minutes until tender.

Serves 4

Sprouted Bean and Mango Salad

🍴 **Hands-on time:** 15 minutes

3 tbsp mango chutney

grated zest and juice of 1 lime

2 tbsp olive oil

4 plum tomatoes

1 small red onion, chopped

1 red pepper, seeded and finely diced

1 yellow pepper, seeded and finely diced

1 mango, peeled, stoned and finely diced (see page 167)

4 tbsp freshly chopped coriander

150g (5oz) sprouted beans (see Save Money)

salt and freshly ground black pepper

1 To make the dressing, place the mango chutney in a small bowl and add the lime zest and juice. Whisk in the oil and season.

2 Quarter the tomatoes, discard the seeds and then cut into dice. Put into a large bowl with the onion, diced peppers, mango, coriander and sprouted beans. Pour the dressing over and mix well. Serve the salad immediately.

SAVE MONEY

Many beans and seeds can be sprouted at home, but buy ones that are specifically produced for sprouting. Mung beans take five to six days to sprout. Allow 125g (4oz) bean sprouts per person. Rinse and drain. Boil or steam for 30 seconds, or stir-fry for 1–2 minutes.

Serves 6

Cod Steaks with Fennel

Hands-on time: 10 minutes, plus marinating
Cooking time: about 20 minutes

1 tbsp hoisin sauce

4 tbsp light soy sauce

4 tbsp dry vermouth

4 tbsp orange juice

½ tsp Chinese five-spice powder

½ tsp ground cumin

1 garlic clove, crushed

4 × 150g (5oz) thick cod fillets or steaks (see Save Effort)

1 tbsp vegetable oil, plus extra to oil the griddle

2 fennel bulbs, about 700g (1½lb), thinly sliced and tops put to one side

2 tsp sesame seeds

1 For the marinade, combine the hoisin sauce, soy sauce, vermouth, orange juice, five-spice powder, cumin and garlic. Put the cod into a shallow dish and pour the marinade over it. Cover and leave to marinate in a cool place for at least 1 hour.

2 Preheat the grill or a lightly oiled griddle. Remove the fish and put the marinade to one side. Cook the fish under the hot grill or on the hot griddle for 4 minutes, then turn it over and cook for a further 3–4 minutes until cooked.

SAVE EFFORT

Ask your fishmonger to remove the scales from the cod's skin. When grilled, the skin will be crisp and delicious to eat.

Serves 4

3 Heat the oil in a sauté pan. Add the fennel and cook briskly for 5–7 minutes until brown and beginning to soften. Add the marinade, bring to the boil and bubble until reduced and sticky.

4 Put the fish on a bed of fennel, spoon any pan juices around it and sprinkle with the sesame seeds. Garnish with the reserved fennel tops and serve.

Crispy Crumbed Fish

Hands-on time: 5 minutes
Cooking time: about 15 minutes

50g (2oz) fresh breadcrumbs
a small handful of freshly chopped
   flat-leafed parsley
2 tbsp capers, chopped
grated zest of 1 lemon
4 haddock or pollack fillets, about 150g
   (5oz) each
½ tbsp Dijon mustard
juice of ½ lemon
salt and freshly ground black pepper
new potatoes and mixed salad to serve

1 Preheat the oven to 180°C (160°C fan oven) mark 4. Put the breadcrumbs into a bowl with the parsley, capers and lemon zest and mix well, then put to one side.

2 Put the fish fillets on a baking tray. Mix the mustard and half the lemon juice in a bowl with a little salt and ground black pepper, then spread over the top of each piece of fish. Spoon the breadcrumb mixture on top – don't worry if some falls off.

3 Cook in the oven for 10–15 minutes until the fish is cooked and the breadcrumbs are golden. Pour the remaining lemon juice over the top and serve with new potatoes and a mixed salad.

SAVE EFFORT

For an easy way to get a brand new recipe, try other fish such as sea bass, sea bream or gurnard.

Chicken Tarragon Sweet Potatoes

Hands-on time: 15 minutes
Cooking time: about 40 minutes

1 tbsp vegetable oil, plus extra for potatoes
4 large sweet potatoes
1 tbsp plain flour
250ml (8fl oz) semi-skimmed milk
½ tbsp wholegrain mustard
2 skinless cooked chicken breasts, sliced
1 fresh tarragon sprig, finely chopped, plus extra to garnish
50g (2oz) baby spinach leaves
salt and freshly ground black pepper
green vegetables or a salad to serve

1 Preheat the oven to 220°C (200°C fan oven) mark 7. Rub a little oil over the sweet potatoes, then put them on a baking tray and cook for 35–40 minutes until cooked (a knife should go through a potato easily).

2 About 10 minutes before the end of the potato cooking time, make the chicken sauce. Heat the oil in a small pan over a medium heat, then stir in the flour and cook for 1 minute. Remove from the heat and gradually whisk in the milk until smooth. Put back on the heat and bring to the boil, whisking all the time. Reduce the heat and simmer the sauce for 3 minutes, then whisk in the mustard and add the chicken. Cook for 2–3 minutes until the chicken is piping hot, then stir in the tarragon and spinach. Check the seasoning.

3 Take the sweet potatoes out of the oven and split them lengthways (don't cut all the way through). Pull the halves gently apart and divide the filling equally among the potatoes. Serve with green vegetables or a salad.

Serves 4

Zesty Turkey One-pan

Hands-on time: 10 minutes
Cooking time: about 10 minutes

½ tbsp olive oil

4 turkey breast steaks, total weight about 500g (1lb 2oz)

350ml (12fl oz) chicken stock

grated zest and juice of 2 lemons

25g (1oz) capers, rinsed and chopped

4 tomatoes, roughly chopped

a large handful of fresh curly parsley, roughly chopped

salt and freshly ground black pepper

boiled rice, seasonal vegetables or salad to serve

1 Heat the oil in a large frying pan over a high heat and fry the turkey steaks for 2 minutes, turning once, to brown the steaks. Add the stock, lemon zest and juice, the capers, tomatoes and some seasoning. Simmer for 8 minutes or until the turkey is cooked through.

2 Add the parsley and check the seasoning. Serve with boiled rice, seasonal vegetables or salad.

SAVE EFFORT

For an easy way to get a brand new recipe, make this zingy supper with chicken, white fish fillets or even prawns.

Serves 4

Steak and Asparagus Stir-fry

Hands-on time: 10 minutes
Cooking time: about 10 minutes

1 × 225g (8oz) rump steak, trimmed
  and sliced

2 tbsp runny honey

2 tbsp teriyaki sauce

1 tbsp sesame oil

150g (5oz) tenderstem broccoli, cut
  into 5cm (2in) lengths

150g (5oz) asparagus, cut into 5cm
  (2in) lengths

75g (3oz) water chestnuts

1 tbsp sesame seeds

salt and freshly ground black pepper

boiled brown rice to serve

1 Put the steak, honey, teriyaki sauce
  and sesame oil into a bowl. Stir and
  leave to marinate for 5 minutes.

2 Heat a wok over a high heat. Lift
  the beef out of the marinade
  (reserving the mixture) and stir-fry
  for 3 minutes until caramelised and
  cooked to medium (cook for longer
  or shorter, if you like). Empty the
  beef into a clean bowl and put to
  one side.

3 Return the wok to the heat and add
  the broccoli, asparagus and a splash
  of water. Fry for 3 minutes or until
  the vegetables are just tender. Stir in
  the marinade, water chestnuts and
  beef and heat for 30 seconds. Check
  the seasoning. Sprinkle the sesame
  seeds over and serve immediately
  with boiled brown rice.

HEALTHY TIP

Sesame seeds are deliciously
nutty and highly nutritious. They
are a valuable source of protein,
good omega fats and vitamin E.

Serves 4

Week 4 - Shopping List

CHILLED & FROZEN

- ❑ 225g (8oz) rump steak
- ❑ 2 skinless cooked chicken breasts
- ❑ 4 × 150g (5oz) haddock or pollack fillets
- ❑ 4 × 150g (5oz) thick cod fillets or steaks
- ❑ 250ml (8fl oz) semi-skimmed milk

FRUIT, VEG & HERBS

- ❑ 1 small red onion
- ❑ 1 garlic clove
- ❑ 1 red pepper
- ❑ 1 yellow pepper
- ❑ 4 large sweet potatoes
- ❑ 4 plum tomatoes
- ❑ 3 carrots
- ❑ 4 tomatoes
- ❑ 150g (5oz) asparagus
- ❑ 150g (5oz) tenderstem broccoli
- ❑ 1 broccoli head
- ❑ 2 fennel bulbs
- ❑ 1 pack of spinach
- ❑ 50g (2oz) baby spinach leaves
- ❑ 150g (5oz) sprouted beans
- ❑ 4 lemons
- ❑ 2 limes
- ❑ 1 mango
- ❑ Fresh root ginger
- ❑ Pack of fresh coriander
- ❑ Pack of fresh flat-leafed parsley
- ❑ Pack of fresh curly parsley
- ❑ Pack of fresh tarragon
- ❑ New potatoes, to serve
- ❑ Mixed salad, to serve
- ❑ Seasonal veg, to serve

STORECUPBOARD

(Here's a checklist in case you need
to re-stock)

- ❑ Vegetable oil
- ❑ Olive oil
- ❑ Sesame oil
- ❑ Chicken stock
- ❑ Plain flour
- ❑ Dijon mustard
- ❑ Wholegrain mustard
- ❑ Hoisin sauce
- ❑ Light soy sauce
- ❑ Teriyaki sauce
- ❑ Red Thai curry paste
- ❑ Mango chutney
- ❑ 75g (3oz) water chestnuts
- ❑ Capers
- ❑ 400ml can coconut milk
- ❑ Chinese five-spice powder
- ❑ Ground cumin
- ❑ 50g (2oz) cashew nuts
- ❑ Sesame seeds
- ❑ Fresh breadcrumbs
- ❑ Runny honey
- ❑ Dry vermouth
- ❑ Orange juice
- ❑ Brown rice, to serve
- ❑ Basmati rice, to serve

Great Dishes
to Share

Take 5 Easy Steps to Health

1. Water

Water is the elixir of life, and is nature's prime detoxifier.

- Aim to drink at least 1 litre (1¾ pints) per day, preferably 1–2 litres (1¾–3½ pints).
- Start the day with a glass of hot water and lemon.
- Have a small bottle or a large glass of mineral or filtered water by your side always, and sip regularly.
- Drinking water at room temperature is easier on the digestion than ice-cold water.
- Bored with plain water? Flavour your water with a slice of lemon, lime or some peeled and chopped fresh ginger.

2. Superfoods

For tip top nutrition and long-term health, incorporate these foods into your regular eating plan:

- ❑ Avocado
- ❑ Broccoli
- ❑ Carrots
- ❑ Cabbage
- ❑ Garlic
- ❑ Ripe tomatoes
- ❑ Sprouted seeds: for example, alfalfa
- ❑ Watercress
- ❑ Winter squash (dense orange-fleshed varieties such as butternut)
- ❑ Apples
- ❑ Apricots
- ❑ Bananas
- ❑ Berries
- ❑ Kiwi fruit
- ❑ Lemons
- ❑ Pineapple
- ❑ Live, natural yogurt
- ❑ Miso
- ❑ Oats
- ❑ Sea vegetables (seaweed): for example, nori strips

3. Good fats and oils

Fats are essential to all life processes, including the production of cholesterol, which is vital for nerve communication and an essential component of the brain, nerve fibres and sex hormones. For this reason, a low-fat diet is not a good idea for long-term health. The trick is to substitute 'bad' (processed, hydrogenated and highly saturated) fats with omega-rich 'good' fats and oils, found in oily fish, nuts and seeds, and to eat small amounts of other natural fats such as olive oil and butter.

- Eat 1–2 tbsp extra virgin (cold pressed) oils every day. Olive oil, hemp, linseed and blends of omega oils are especially good. Do not heat. Use them to drizzle over salads, vegetables and fish, and in dips.

4. Vegetables, salads and fruit

Vegetables, salads and fruit are star performers in all healthy eating plans, including low-GI ones. Not only do they contain a storehouse of vitamins and minerals, they also help to keep the body at its optimum pH, which is slightly alkaline.

5. Eat regularly

Skipping meals leads to energy dips, stresses your system and is a sure-fire way to put on weight. Eating regularly keeps your body's physical and mental energy levels steady, avoiding hunger pangs and the need to snack.

- Never skip breakfast – it's the most important meal of the day to set you up and it also sustains your energy levels through until lunchtime.
- Eat slowly and take your time – it takes 20 minutes for your body to register it is full and satiated.

Perfect Mussels

One of the most popular shellfish, mussels takes moments to cook.
Careful preparation is important, so give yourself enough time to
get the shellfish ready.

Cooking mussels

1 Scrape off the fibres attached to
the shells (beards). If the mussels
are very clean, give them a quick
rinse under the cold tap. If they
are very sandy, scrub them with
a stiff brush.

2 If the shells have sizeable barnacles
on them, it is best (though not
essential) to remove them. Rap
them sharply with a metal spoon
or the back of a washing-up brush,
then scrape off.

3 Discard any open mussels that
don't shut when sharply tapped;
this means they are dead and could
be dangerous to eat.

1

4 In a large heavy-based pan, fry 2 finely chopped shallots and a generous handful of parsley in 25g (1oz) butter for about 2 minutes or until soft. Pour in 1cm (½in) dry white wine.

5 Add the mussels to the pan and cover tightly with a lid. Steam for 5–10 minutes until the shells open. Immediately take the pan away from the heat.

6 Using a slotted spoon, remove the mussels from the pan and discard any that haven't opened, then boil the cooking liquid rapidly to reduce. Pour over the mussels and serve immediately.

Smoky Spanish Mussels

Hands-on time: 25 minutes
Cooking time: about 20 minutes

2kg (4½lb) fresh mussels, scrubbed, rinsed and beards removed (see Save Effort)

2 tsp olive oil

1 onion, thinly sliced

2 red peppers, seeded and thinly sliced

1 garlic clove, thinly sliced

½ tsp smoked paprika

pinch of saffron threads

500ml (17fl oz) fish stock

a large handful of fresh parsley leaves, chopped

crusty bread to serve (optional)

1 Sort the mussels following the instructions on the previous page. Clean under running water, removing any barnacles or beards.

2 Heat the oil in a very large pan (which has a tight-fitting lid) over a medium heat. Fry the onion and peppers for 10 minutes or until softened. Add the garlic, paprika and saffron and fry for 1 minute more. Stir in the stock and half the parsley and bring to the boil.

3 Tip the sorted and cleaned mussels into the pan. Cover and simmer, shaking occasionally, for 5 minutes or until the mussels have fully opened (discard any that remain closed). Divide among four large bowls, scatter the remaining parsley over and serve immediately with some crusty bread, if you like.

SAVE EFFORT

Try to buy rope-grown mussels – they're easier to clean.

Serves 4

Mushroom and Two-grain Risotto

Hands-on time: 20 minutes
Cooking time: about 25 minutes

200g (7oz) risotto rice, such as arborio or carnaroli

100g (3½oz) quinoa

1.1 litres (2 pints) vegetable stock

25g (1oz) butter

1 onion, finely chopped

250g pack chestnut mushrooms, sliced

4 fresh thyme sprigs, leaves picked

2 garlic cloves, crushed

a large handful of fresh rocket

salt and freshly ground black pepper

Parmesan shavings to serve (optional)

1 Put the rice and quinoa into a large pan. Add the stock and bring to the boil. Reduce the heat to a gentle simmer, then cook, stirring frequently, until tender and thickened – about 20 minutes.

2 Meanwhile, heat the butter in a separate large frying pan and gently cook the onion for 10 minutes or until soft. Increase the heat to high and add the mushrooms. Cook, stirring frequently, for 5 minutes or until tender and any moisture has evaporated. Add the thyme leaves, garlic and some seasoning and cook for 1 minute more. Take off the heat and put to one side.

3 When the rice mixture is ready, stir the mushroom mixture and most of the rocket through it. Check the seasoning and divide among four bowls. To serve, garnish with the remaining rocket and, if you like, top with Parmesan shavings; serve immediately.

Serves 4

Skinny Bean Tacos

Hands-on time: 15 minutes
Cooking time: about 10 minutes

---

2 × 400g cans chopped tomatoes

2 tsp runny honey

410g can cannellini beans, drained and rinsed

400g can kidney beans, drained and rinsed

198g can sweetcorn, drained

1 red onion, finely chopped

salt and freshly ground black pepper

To serve

8 corn tacos

reduced-fat guacamole,

a large handful of parsley leaves, chopped

1 Put the tomatoes into a medium pan with the honey and plenty of seasoning. Bring to the boil, then reduce the heat and simmer until thickened – about 8 minutes.

2 Stir in both types of beans, the sweetcorn, onion and some seasoning. Heat through and check the seasoning.

3 Warm the taco shells according to the pack instructions.

4 Put the bean mixture, tacos, guacamole and parsley into separate bowls, take to the table and let everyone serve themselves.

SAVE EFFORT

For an easy way to get a brand new recipe, fry some turkey mince separately and stir into the mixture in step 2.

Serves 4

Turkey Meatballs with Barbecue Sauce

Hands-on time: 15 minutes
Cooking time: about 20 minutes

500g (1lb 2oz) turkey mince

2 tsp ground coriander

½–1 red chilli, seeded and finely chopped (see Safety Tip, page 68)

½ tbsp olive oil

1 onion, finely chopped

1 garlic clove, crushed

400g can chopped tomatoes

2 tbsp soy sauce

3 tbsp tomato ketchup

salt and freshly ground black pepper

fresh coriander, chives or parsley to garnish

boiled wholegrain rice to serve

1 Preheat the oven to 200°C (180°C fan oven) mark 6 and line a baking tray with baking parchment.

2 Put the turkey mince into a large bowl, add the ground coriander, chilli and plenty of seasoning and mix through (using your hands is easiest). Form into walnut-sized meatballs – you should have about 20.

3 Arrange the meatballs on the prepared tray and cook in the oven, turning midway, for 20 minutes or until golden and cooked through.

4 Meanwhile, heat the oil in a large pan over a medium heat. Add the onion and fry for 10 minutes or until softened. Stir in the garlic and cook for 1 minute, then add the tomatoes, soy sauce, ketchup and seasoning. Bring to the boil, then reduce the heat and simmer for 10 minutes or until thickened slightly.

5 Add the meatballs to the sauce and stir gently to coat. Garnish with fresh herbs and serve with boiled wholegrain rice.

Serves 4

Harissa Chicken and Couscous Salad

🍴 **Hands-on time:** 25 minutes
Cooking time: about 25 minutes

1 tbsp rose harissa paste
4 skinless chicken breasts
1 litre (1¾ pints) chicken stock
200g (7oz) giant wholewheat couscous
½ courgette, finely chopped
100g (3½oz) cherry tomatoes,
  quartered
2 spring onions, finely sliced
40g (1½oz) feta cheese, crumbled
a large handful of fresh coriander
  leaves, roughly chopped
salt and freshly ground black pepper
tzatziki to serve (optional)

1 Preheat the oven to 200°C (180°C
fan oven) mark 6. Rub harissa paste
over the chicken breasts and put
them on a baking tray. Roast for
20–25 minutes until cooked through.

2 Meanwhile, bring the stock to
the boil in a large pan. Add the
couscous and simmer according to
the pack instructions or until tender
– about 8 minutes. Drain.

3 Transfer the couscous to a large
platter, add the courgette, tomatoes,
onions, cheese, coriander and some
seasoning and mix through.

4 Carefully slice the cooked chicken
and lay on top of the couscous salad.
Serve warm or at room temperature,
with tzatziki, if you like.

HEALTHY TIP

The tomatoes are full of vitamin
C, which is a powerful antioxidant
and anti-viral nutrient crucial for a
healthy immune system.

Serves 4

Quick Turkey and Pork Stir-fry

Hands-on time: 15 minutes
Cooking time: about 10 minutes

1 tbsp vegetable oil

200g (7oz) turkey breast, cut into finger-sized strips

200g (7oz) pork loin fillet, cut into finger-sized strips

1 tbsp Chinese five-spice powder

1 each yellow and orange pepper, seeded and sliced

150g (5oz) pak choi, thickly shredded

1 tsp sesame seeds

1–1½ tbsp soy sauce, to taste

a large handful of fresh coriander

noodles or boiled rice to serve (optional)

1 Heat the oil in a large wok or frying pan over a high heat and add the turkey and pork. Cook for 3 minutes, stirring occasionally. Add the five-spice powder, sliced peppers, pak choi and a splash of water.

2 Continue to cook for a few minutes until the vegetables are just tender (but retaining a crunch) and the meat is cooked through (add more water as needed).

3 Sprinkle the sesame seeds over, add the soy sauce and rip in the coriander. Check the seasoning and serve with noodles or boiled rice, if you like.

HEALTHY TIP

The pak choi provides valuable A and C vitamins.

Serves 4

Creamy Prawn and Pea Penne

Hands-on time: 15 minutes
Cooking time: about 15 minutes

300g (11oz) wholewheat penne pasta

150g (5oz) frozen peas

½ tbsp oil

2 medium leeks, thinly sliced

1 garlic clove, crushed

300g (11oz) cooked peeled king prawns

zest and juice of 1 lemon

100g (3½oz) 2% fat Greek yogurt

salt and freshly ground black pepper

1 Bring a large pan of salted water to the boil and cook the pasta according to the pack instructions, adding the peas for the final 2 minutes of cooking.

2 Meanwhile, heat the oil in a large frying pan and gently cook the leeks for 10 minutes, then add the garlic and prawns and cook for 2 minutes or until the prawns are heated through. Stir in the lemon zest and Greek yogurt.

3 When the pasta and peas are cooked to your liking, reserve one cupful of the cooking water, then drain. Stir the pasta and peas into the leek mixture. Add enough of the reserved pasta water to make a smooth sauce. Season well, adding lemon juice to taste. Serve immediately.

HEALTHY TIP

Leeks are an excellent source of vitamin C, as well as iron and fibre.

Sausage and Gnocchi One-pan

Hands-on time: 20 minutes
Cooking time: about 25 minutes

1 tsp vegetable oil
2 large pork sausages
1 red onion, finely sliced
1 fat garlic clove, crushed
150g (5oz) gnocchi
2 × 410g cans cannellini beans, drained and rinsed
400ml (14fl oz) chicken stock
a large handful of baby spinach leaves or fresh parsley
salt and freshly ground black pepper
crusty bread to serve (optional)

1 Heat the oil in a large, deep frying pan and fry the sausages and onion until golden.

2 Stir in the garlic, gnocchi, cannellini beans, stock and plenty of seasoning. Bring to the boil, then reduce the heat and simmer for 10–15 minutes until the sausages are cooked through.

3 Lift the sausages out of the mixture and slice into 1cm (½in) thick slices. Return the slices to the pan and fold the spinach or parsley through. Check the seasoning and serve, with some crusty bread to mop up the juices, if you like.

HEALTHY TIP

You can still enjoy higher-fat ingredients, like sausages, but make them go further by bulking the dish up with healthier alternatives.

Serves 4

Vitality Drinks

Making Smoothies and Purées

Fruit, whether cooked or raw, can be transformed into a smooth sauce by puréeing. It also makes a healthy breakfast or snack that is bursting with flavour when used in a smoothie.

Making smoothies

To serve four, you will need:
4 passion fruit, 150ml (¼ pint) low-fat yogurt, 4 bananas, 225g (8oz) grapes.

1 Halve the passion fruit and scoop the pulp into a blender. Add the remaining ingredients. Crush 8 ice cubes and add to the blender.
2 Process until smooth and pour into glasses. Serve immediately.

Puréeing in a blender

Some fruit can be puréed raw, while others are better cooked. Wait until cooked fruit cools.

1 Blend a spoonful of fruit until smooth, then add another spoonful and blend. Add rest of fruit in batches.

2 For a very smooth purée, pass through a fine sieve.

Busy Bee's Comforter

🍴 **Hands-on time:** 5 minutes

2 lemons

150g (5oz) full-fat natural or soya
  yogurt, at room temperature

1–2 tsp thick honey

2–3 tsp bee pollen grains or equivalent
  in capsule form (see Health Tip)

1 Using a sharp knife, cut off the peel
  from one lemon, removing as much
  of the white pith as possible. Chop
  the flesh roughly, discarding any
  pips, and put into a blender. Squeeze
  the juice from the remaining lemon
  and add to the blender.

2 Spoon in the yogurt and whiz until
  smooth. Taste and sweeten with
  honey as necessary. Stir in the bee
  pollen, then pour into a glass and
  serve immediately.

HEALTHY TIP

You can buy bee pollen grains
at specialist health food shops
and online.

This drink is a very good source
of protein and calcium. It contains
honey, which is a source of slow-
releasing sugars and a powerful
antibacterial and anti-viral
ingredient.

This drink is not suitable for those
with an allergy to pollen, such as
hayfever sufferers.

SAVE EFFORT

For an easy way to get a brand
new recipe, use oranges instead
of lemons.

Serves 1, makes 200ml (7fl oz)

Strawberry and Camomile Comforter

Hands-on time: 5 minutes, plus infusing and cooling

2 camomile teabags
5cm (2in) piece cinnamon stick
175g (6oz) strawberries
150ml (¼ pint) freshly pressed apple
   juice or 2 large dessert apples, juiced

1 Put the teabags and cinnamon stick
   into a small heatproof jug and pour
   in 150ml (¼ pint) boiling water.
   Leave to infuse for 5 minutes, then
   discard the bags and cinnamon
   stick. Leave to cool.
2 When ready to serve, remove the
   hulls from the strawberries, then
   wash and pat dry the fruit with
   kitchen paper. Put into a blender.
3 Pour in the apple juice and cold
   camomile tea and whiz for a few
   seconds until smooth. Pour into two
   tall glasses and serve.

SAVE EFFORT

Camomile teabags are very
convenient and easy to use, but
freshly dried camomile flowers
will give a stronger flavour.

Serves 2, makes 600ml (1 pint)

Fruity Carrot with Ginger

Hands-on time: 10 minutes

2 medium oranges

1cm (½in) piece fresh root ginger,
    peeled and roughly chopped

150ml (¼ pint) freshly pressed apple
    juice or 2 dessert apples, juiced

150ml (¼ pint) freshly pressed carrot
    juice or 3 medium carrots, 250g
    (9oz), juiced

mint leaves to decorate

1 Using a sharp knife, cut a slice of
    orange and put to one side for the
    decoration. Cut off the peel from
    the oranges, removing as much
    of the white pith as possible. Chop
    the flesh roughly, discarding any
    pips, and put into a blender. Add
    the ginger.

2 Pour in the apple and carrot juice
    and blend until smooth. Divide
    between two glasses, decorate with
    quartered orange slices and a mint
    leaf and serve.

HEALTHY TIP

This drink is full of vitamin C
and betacarotene, an antioxidant
that helps combat harmful
free radicals and promotes
healthy skin), making it a great
immunity-boosting supplement.
Fresh ginger is good for calming
an upset stomach and providing
relief from bloating and gas.

Serves 2, makes 600ml (1 pint)

Raspberry Rascal Booster

Hands-on time: 5 minutes

225g (8oz) raspberries, thawed if
  frozen, juices reserved

1 medium orange

2 tsp thick honey

1 If using fresh raspberries, remove
the hulls, then wash and pat the
fruit dry with kitchen paper. Put
two raspberries to one side for
decoration and put the rest into a
blender. If the fruit has been frozen,
add the juices as well.

2 Peel the orange, removing as much
of the white pith as possible. Chop
the flesh roughly, discarding any
pips, and put into the blender. Add
the honey and whiz until smooth,
then pour into a glass, decorate
with the raspberries and serve
immediately.

HEALTHY TIP

This drink is bursting with
vitamin C and anthocyanins,
which help strengthen blood
vessels and boost your immune
system.
If you find this smoothie too
thick, water it down a little.

Serves 1, makes 300ml (½ pint)

Take 5 Breakfast Smoothie

TAKE 5

🍴 **Hands-on time:** 5 minutes

200ml (7fl oz) semi-skimmed milk

200g (7oz) natural yogurt

125g (4oz) mix of frozen berries, such as blackberries, blueberries and blackcurrants

15g (½oz) rolled oats

2 tbsp runny honey

1 Put all the ingredients into a blender and whiz until smooth. Pour into two tall glasses and serve.

SAVE TIME

If you prefer to have your breakfast ready to go, make a double smoothie batch in the evening, then transfer the mixture to a jug, cover and chill for up to two days. Simply stir before serving.

Serves 2

Creamy Dairy-free Banana

Hands-on time: 5 minutes

1 large ripe banana

125g (4oz) silken tofu, well chilled (see Save Money)

175ml (6fl oz) unsweetened soya milk, well chilled

2 tsp thick honey

a few drops of vanilla extract

1 Peel the banana and slice thickly. Put into a blender.

2 Drain the tofu, mash lightly with a fork and add to the blender.

3 Pour in the milk and add the honey with a few drops of vanilla extract. Whiz for a few seconds until thick and smooth. Pour into a large glass and serve.

SAVE MONEY

Silken tofu is very smooth and is the best for blending in drinks. It is available fresh or vacuum-packed in cartons. Firmer types can be used but give a grainier texture when blended.

Serves 1, makes 400ml (14fl oz)

Pineapples

1. Cut off the base and crown of the pineapple and stand the fruit on a chopping board.
2. Using a medium-sized knife, peel away a section of skin, going just deep enough to remove all or most of the hard, inedible 'eyes' on the skin. Repeat all the way around.
3. Use a small knife to cut out any remaining traces of the eyes.
4. Cut the peeled pineapple into slices.
5. You can buy special tools for coring pineapples but a 7.5cm (3in) biscuit cutter or an apple corer works just as well. Place the biscuit cutter directly over the core and press down firmly. If using an apple corer, cut out the core in pieces, as it will be too wide to remove in one piece.

Mangos

1. Cut a slice to one side in the centre. Repeat on the other side.
2. Cut parallel lines into the flesh of one slice, almost to the skin. Cut another set of lines to cut the flesh into squares.
3. Press on the skin to turn the fruit inside out, so that the flesh is thrust outwards. Cut off the chunks as close as possible to the skin. Repeat with the other half.

Mango and Oat Smoothie

Hands-on time: 5 minutes

150g (5oz) natural yogurt
1 small mango, peeled, stoned and
   chopped (see page 167)
2 tbsp oats
4 ice cubes

1 Put the yogurt into a blender. Put a
   little chopped mango to one side
   for the decoration, if you like, and
   add the remaining mango, the oats
   and ice cubes to the yogurt. Whiz
   until smooth. Serve immediately,
   decorated with chopped mango.

HEALTHY TIP

This oaty drink will help
satisfy hunger for relatively few
calories. The fibre in oats helps
stabilise blood sugar levels,
lower cholesterol and control the
appetite. Mangoes add lots of
betacarotene (see page 158).

SAVE EFFORT

For an easy way to get a brand
new recipe, instead of mango,
use 2 nectarines or peaches, or
175g (6oz) soft seasonal fruits
such as raspberries, strawberries
or blueberries.

Serves 2

364 cal ♥ 15g protein
9g fat (2g sat) ♥ 8g fibre
55g carb ♥ 2.1g salt

12

279 cal ♥ 10g protein
6g fat (1g sat) ♥ 5g fibre
49g carb ♥ 0.2g salt

14

208 cal ♥ 7g protein
9g fat (trace sat) ♥ 3g fibre
28g carb ♥ 0g salt

16

193 cal ♥ 9g protein
8g fat (1g sat) ♥ 2g fibre
22g carb ♥ 0.3g salt

20

187 cal ♥ 3g protein
1g fat (0g sat) ♥ 6g fibre
47g carb ♥ 0.1g salt

30

192 cal ♥ 4g protein ♥ 1g fat
(trace sat) ♥ 3g fibre
45g carb ♥ 0.1g salt

32

with 1 slice of cornbread
359 cal ♥ 25g protein
4g fat (1g sat) ♥ 6g fibre
64g carb ♥ 1.3g salt

38

256 cal ♥ 29g protein
10g fat (5g sat) ♥ 6g fibre
14g carb ♥ 0.4g salt

50

240 cal ♥ 16g protein
9g fat (2g sat) ♥ 3g fibre
25g carb ♥ 1.6g salt

52

205 cal ♥ 37g protein
4g fat (1g sat) ♥ 0.6g fibre
12g carb ♥ 0.4g salt

54

142 cal ♥ 15g protein
3g fat (1g sat) ♥ 2g fibre
16g carb ♥ 0.2g salt

70

271 cal ♥ 40g protein
7g fat (2g sat) ♥ 2g fibre
12g carb ♥ 0.8g salt

72

132 cal ♥ 32g protein
2g fat (0g sat) ♥ 0.7g fibre
4g carb ♥ 1.4g salt

74

280 cal ♥ 22g protein
7g fat (2g sat) ♥ 3g fibre
34g carb ♥ 0.8g salt

76

145 cal ♥ 11g protein
1g fat (0g sat) ♥ 5g fibre
30g carb ♥ 0.4g salt

188 cal ♥ 4g protein
7g fat (1g sat) ♥ 3g fibre
29g carb ♥ 0g salt

236 cal ♥ 4g protein
9g fat (4g sat) ♥ 1g fibre
37g carb ♥ 0.5g salt

156 cal ♥ 1g protein ♥ 0g fat
2g fibre ♥ 40g carb ♥ 0g salt

137 cal ♥ 14g protein
9g fat (5g sat) ♥ 3g fibre
5g carb ♥ 0.4g salt

without sour cream or
guacamole 375 cal ♥ 36g
protein ♥ 8g fat (2g sat) ♥ 5g
fibre ♥ 41g carb ♥ 2g salt

188 cal ♥ 28g protein
3g fat (0g sat) ♥ 4g fibre
13g carb ♥ 1.8g salt

334 cal ♥ 18g protein
8g fat (2g sat) ♥ 2g fibre
51g carb ♥ 3.5g salt

268 cal ♥ 35g protein
g fat (trace sat) ♥ 2g fibre
37g carb ♥ 0.4g salt

214 cal ♥ 12g protein
7g fat (1g sat) ♥ 10g fibre
29g carb ♥ 0.2g salt

280 cal ♥ 10g protein
10g fat (1g sat) ♥ 7g fibre
34g carb ♥ 1.3g salt

168 cal ♥ 20g protein
7g fat (1g sat) ♥ 1g fibre
8g carb ♥ 0.2g salt

298 cal ♥ 11g protein
4g fat (1g sat) ♥ 56g fibre
0.8g carb ♥ 8g salt

249 cal ♥ 10g protein
9g fat (4g sat) ♥ 1g fibre
31g carb ♥ 0.9g salt

164 cal ♥ 5g protein
8g fat (1g sat) ♥ 9g fibre
22g carb ♥ 2g salt

223 cal ♥ 12g protein
10g fat (2g sat) ♥ 2g fibre
22g carb ♥ 1.4g salt

371 cal ♥ 25g protein;
5g fat (1g sat) ♥ 5g fibre
43g carb ♥ 5g salt

88

223 cal ♥ 17g protein
6g fat (2g sat) ♥ 1g fibre
30g carb ♥ 0.2g salt

90

331cal ♥ 28g protein;
8g fat (2g sat) ♥ 1g fibre
37g carb ♥ 2g salt

92

393 cal ♥ 15g protein
9g fat (4g sat) ♥ 3g fibre
66g carb ♥ 0.3g salt

96

201 cal ♥ 44g protein
2g fat (1g sat) ♥ 0.2g fibre
7g carb ♥ 0.5g salt

106

207 cal ♥ 23g protein
10g fat (3g sat) ♥ 2g fibre
4g carb ♥ 2g salt

108

200 cal ♥ 6g protein
10g fat (2g sat) ♥ 5g fibre
19g carb ♥ 0.7g salt

112

103 cal ♥ 2g protein
4g fat (1g sat) ♥ 3g fibre
15g carb ♥ 0.1g salt

114

188 cal ♥ 15g protein
7g fat (2g sat) ♥ 2g fibre
15g carb ♥ 0.1g salt

124

193 cal ♥ 24g protein
5g fat (1g sat) ♥ 2g fibre
13g carb ♥ 1.2g salt

134

342 cal ♥ 9g protein
8g fat (4g sat) ♥ 1g fibre
61g carb ♥ 2g salt

136

309 cal ♥ 14g protein
8g fat (3g sat) ♥ 11g fibre
51g carb ♥ 3g salt

138

306 cal ♥ 13g protein
8g fat (2g sat) ♥ 10g fibre
44g carb ♥ 2.3g salt

148

130 cal ♥ 10g protein
2g fat (1g sat) ♥ 8g fibre
24g carb ♥ 0.3g salt

154

52 cal ♥ 0.9g protein
trace fat ♥ 1g fibre
13g carb ♥ 0g salt

156

128 cal ♥ 3g protein
1g fat (trace sat) ♥ 3g fibre
30g carb ♥ 0.1g salt

158

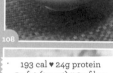

177 cal ♥ 13g protein
g fat (3g sat) ♥ 1g fibre
16g carb ♥ 1.3g salt

282 cal ♥ 29g protein;
7g fat (1g sat) ♥ 4g fibre
29g carb ♥ 1.3g salt

3 skewers ♥ 153 cal
14g protein ♥ 2g fat (0.3g sat)
2g fibre ♥ 19g carb ♥ 0.8g salt

273 cal ♥ 42g protein
7g fat (2g sat) ♥ 3g fibre
9g carb ♥ 1g salt

209 cal ♥ 30g protein
g fat (1g sat) ♥ 4g fibre
6g carb ♥ 1.4g salt

171 cal ♥ 30g protein
1g fat (trace sat) ♥ 0.3g fibre
10g carb ♥ 0.8g salt

203 cal ♥ 44g protein
4g fat (1g sat) ♥ 0.9g fibre
3g carb ♥ 1g salt

363 cal ♥ 25g protein
7g fat (2g sat) ♥ 6g fibre
54g carb ♥ 1g salt

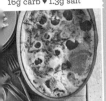

281 cal ♥ 37g protein
g fat (3g sat) ♥ 0.8g fibre
10g carb ♥ 1.3g salt

346 cal ♥ 44g protein
7g fat (3g sat) ♥ 0.4g fibre
28g carb ♥ 3g salt

264 cal ♥ 30g protein
8g fat (2g sat) ♥ 2g fibre
6g carb ♥ 0.2g salt

392 cal ♥ 30g protein
5g fat (1g sat) ♥ 9g fibre
64g carb ♥ 4g salt

283 cal ♥ 16g protein
8g fat (1g sat) ♥ 2g fibre
25g carb ♥ 0.2g salt

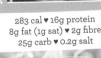

147 cal ♥ 5g protein
1g fat (trace sat) ♥ 8g fibre
33g carb ♥ 0g salt

205 cal ♥ 10g protein
3g fat (2g sat) ♥ 2g fibre
36g carb ♥ 0.3g salt

145 cal ♥ 6g protein
2g fat (1g sat) ♥ 3g fibre
27g carb ♥ 0.2g salt

100

102

104

118

120

122

142

144

146

162

164

168

Index

PICTURE CREDITS
Photographers:
Steve Baxter (page 87);
Martin Brigdale (page 75);
Nicki Dowey (pages 13, 15, 17, 21,
23, 25, 29, 31, 33, 53, 55, 67, 83, 91,
109, 113, 115, 155, 157, 159, 161, 165
and 169); Will Heap (page 69);
Gareth Morgans (pages 49, 77,
85, 89, 93, 99, 101, 103, 105, 107,
121, 123, 125, 135, 137, 139, 141, 143,
145, 147 and 149); Craig Robertson
(pages 27, 41, 56, 57, 65, 71, 81, 119,
132, 133, 152, 153, 166 and 167);
Lucinda Symons (pages 59 and
117); Jon Whitaker (pages 39, 43,
47, 51, 73 and 97); Kate Whitaker
(page 163).

Home Economists:
Anna Burges-Lumsden, Joanna
Farrow, Emma Jane Frost,
Teresa Goldfinch, Alice Hart,
Lucy McKelvie, Kim Morphew,
Aya Nishimura, Bridget Sargeson,
Sarah Tildesley, Jennifer White
and Mari Mererid Williams.

Stylists: Tamzin Ferdinando,
Wei Tang, Sarah Tildesley,
Helen Trent and Fanny Ward.

BAKE ME A CAKE

There's always time for cake

EASY PEASY MEALS

Easy meals for every day

LET'S DO BRUNCH

Mouth-watering meals to start your day

CHEAP EATS

Budget-busting ideas that won't break the bank

SALAD DAYS

Oh-so-fresh ideas for fabulous salads

Available online at store.anovabooks.com and from all good bookshops

POSH NOSH

Delicious recipes to impress your guests

PARTY FOOD

Delicious recipes to get the party started

SLOW STOPPERS

Slow-cooked meals packed with flavour

GREAT VEG

Inspired ideas for delicious veggie meals

AL FRESCO EATS

Easy grills, barbecues and picnics

ROAST IT

There's nothing better than a delicious roast

FLASH IN THE PAN

Spice up your noodles and stir-fries

GLUTEN-FREE AND EASY

Oh-so-good-for-you recipes that taste great

LOW FAT LOW CAL

Nice recipes don't need to be naughty